Your
Staffordshire
Bull Terrier

Raymond

By Steve Bradder

First published 2004
Printed and bound in China through Printworks Int. Ltd.

Contents

Front cover: Ch Domino Flashy Lad. Bred, owned and shown by Steve and Julie Bradder. Photo courtesy of Raymond.

Title page: Ch Rogue Saga Photo courtesy of Raymond

Contents page: Photo courtesy of Raymond

Acknowledgements

For photographs: Alan Raymond, Brian Owen, Alan Walker, David Dalton and Neil Glover.

Foreword

Steve Bradder was born in a small mining town in Nottinghamshire in 1963. Later on his family moved to Newton, a tiny village in Derbyshire. It was at the neighbouring village school, Tibshelf Secondary, where Steve was educated and also met his childhood sweetheart Julie. They married in 1986. Julie is not only Steve's wife but also his partner in the dog game. Together they make quite a team.

Julie was brought up with Staffords from the age of 6. Steve was also surrounded by four-legged friends as a child. Although these were not Staffords (his family preferring Labradors), the bond between man and his best friend had been formed. Soon after their marriage Steve and Julie realised that owning their own dogs was a must.

A visit to see a local litter of Staffordshire Bull Terrier pups resulted in them buying not 1 but 2 of the bitches! They eventually bred from one of these bitches, producing a litter of 5 dogs, including Arnie. Arnie was sold to a friend. From the age of 12 weeks it was obvious that the dog was a bit special. As his breeder, Steve successfully campaigned him on behalf of their friend, Jim. Fate then took a terrible turn. Whilst in hospital for a routine hip operation, Jim suddenly passed away shortly after the operation. This tragedy would change Steve and Julie's lives forever. At the request of Jim's widow, Maureen, Arnie was rehomed to his breeders.

In Jim's memory Steve carried on showing Arnie. He would not only go on to gain his Champion title but also to become the most successful show Stafford the world has ever seen. He became the Breed Record Holder, winning 28 Challenge Certificates and also became the only Stafford in the history of the breed to win Best in Show at The National Terrier Club Championship Show in 1995.

Steve has been showing and breeding Staffords for thirteen years, enjoying success not only with Arnie but with other dogs from the Brajulste kennel. His whole attitude to exhibiting a Staffordshire Bull Terrier - not only the presentation of his stock but also his own personal appearance - has turned a few heads! Steve has proved that a top quality dog coupled with expert handling can make a formidable team which is very hard to beat. This is something we are very proud of in Staffords, that complete newcomers to the breed can campaign very successfully (provided of course their animals are good enough).

On a personal note, I have known Steve for some 20 years now, not only through Staffords, but also from my previous workplace. He is a quiet, unassuming, very nice person to know, whose knowledge certainly belies his years. After all, he has hit heights in Staffords which no one else ever has. You will not find him shouting from the roof tops but, if his advice is required, you will be assured of it. From his humble beginnings, Arnie (Ch Domino Flashy Lad) is now world famous.

When Steve first told me that he had been approached to write a book directly aimed at beginners to the Breed, I could not think of a better person for the job. As you read through this book you will discover that it does not claim to be definitive in any way. It is not a platform to impose hard and fast methods for looking after your new Stafford; it is simply the Brajulste way of doing things.

Finally, just read and enjoy. You'll find Steve's personality and, in particular, his modesty, come shining through. It is a very entertaining and informative read.

Mrs Joan Holmes (Holmestaff Staffords)

Dedication

Dedicated to the memory of our friend Jim Whittaker. Also, special thanks to our late friend, Sam, whose lifetime in dogs and knowledge passed on to us has been priceless. God bless. My mother and father-in-law for all the help and advice. Mrs Joan Holmes for the Foreword.

Preface

When I was first approached about writing about my hobby, namely Staffordshire Bull Terriers, I thought they must have got me mixed up with somebody else! I was asked if I could write something that I would have liked to read when my interest in Staffords first gripped. Something in fact that could be of help to newcomers to the Breed. After quite a lot of thought I decided to give it a go. I cannot begin to tell you how my life has changed over the last 13 years or so. This book is just one example. After many late nights and many very long hours (several times I thought about throwing the towel in as I appeared to be getting nowhere fast), things eventually began to take shape. The book has ended up like a kind of factual novel.

Staffordshire Bull terriers are very special dogs and, if you find yourself reading this, you must be already hooked or very nearly about to be!

Finally, I would like to thank Julie and the rest of my family for giving me the encouragement to stick at it but most of all to Arnie - Champion Domino Flashy Lad. Without his success in the show ring, none of this would have been possible.

I sincerely hope that something in here may be to your assistance.

Testimonials

"It is congratulations to the young owner/handler who did our Breed proud on that never to be forgotten day, 1st April 1995, when a point of note in Stafford history was made. He can claim in modesty that his Stafford is a first at National Terrier and in this award Ch Domino Flashy Lad can never be surpassed."
Bill McKnight

"..... projected now to the top and thus joins the ranks of the elite."

"..... the dog is a credit to the Breed and the way Steve presents both the dog and himself is a lesson to breeders and exhibitors of all breeds."
Robert Killick

CHAPTER 1

HISTORY

Two gorgeous Stafford pups. Note the ears no lower than eye level.

The Staffordshire Bull Terrier has been in existence since the 17th century. It seems that the men of those times tried several crosses, mainly to create a dog that suited their particular interests at the time.

The Staffordshire Bull Terrier was created by people whose only interest was in dog fighting and other blood sports including bull-baiting, bear-baiting and in some cases horse-baiting. The Stafford was then known as the 'Bull and Terrier' or 'Pit Dog'.

Bull-baiting and bear-baiting were outlawed in 1835. With this so-called 'entertainment' being abolished, organised dog fighting started to become more popular. Although just as barbaric as bull-baiting and bear-baiting, dog fighting was still a legal pastime for our forefathers.

To arrive at the desired end product it was decided that the ideal cross would be between the Bulldog and the English White Terrier. The Bulldog for its strength and tenacity and the English White Terrier for its speed and agility.

This is where the early Stafford come into his own. In the 'pit'. When it came to reproducing these fighting dogs, the only criterion that had to be met was basically that the dog had to be 'good in the pit'. The more ferocious the better, in the hope that the dog would pass on his fighting skills to his offspring.

Much as I hate the breed's distant history, it is completely impossible to avoid it. It is why the breed evolved. It is how the breed evolved. It is its history. Love it or hate it, it is there for all to see.

I'd like to think that nowadays we are far more educated and sensible than our forefathers

The Stafford - the ultimate family pet.

of the early 1900s. Dog fighting, although the reason why the Stafford is here today, has been illegal for almost 90 years. Therefore it goes without saying that in today's society there is no need for fighting dogs. The Stafford now is a top class show dog, bred to a specific Kennel Club Standard. There are now only two reasons why the Stafford is here. First and foremost, the ultimate family pet and secondly, the show dog.

It saddens me deeply when I hear comments that today's modern show type Stafford is ruining the breed. Comments like, "Staffords aren't meant to be show dogs, that's for other dogs. Staffords should be in the pit, it's what they were bred for." For Heaven's sake, it's the year 2001, not 1899!

The Dangerous Dogs Act 1991 has made it imperative for everybody connected in any way with Staffords to be ultra-careful. If not, the breed I love will be faced with the same fate as the American Pit Bull Terrier. I will go into greater detail about this Act in chapter 8.

Although I like to see a Stafford showing spirit in the show ring, this is where it must finish. Given the chance, they'll still fight, and right to the death, especially if encouraged.

At this time organised dog fighting was becoming more popular. It was easier to stage a dog fight with things being on a smaller scale compared to the bull and bear baiting exploits. Very often a make-do pit could be put together in a matter of minutes, either with bales of straw or wooden battens. The cellars of pubs were very popular and also barns. In fact, basically anywhere.

This pastime was particularly popular amongst the miners and steelworkers of the Black Country. It was not unusual for an impromptu dog fight to take place between dogs belonging to workmates, each of whom insisted that his dog was the best. Even then, organised dog fighting attracted big money. Wagers of up to £200 have been mentioned. Our forefathers laid down the rules and regulations for the 'sport' of dog fighting, which were subject to variation in different parts of the country.

Dogs were matched by weight, pound for pound. This could range from a lightweight pair of perhaps 12lb each up to the real heavyweights, who could be in the region of 60lb plus.

As well as the rules (see Appendix B), agreements were also drawn up as follows:

Articles of Agreement

Articles of Agreement made on the .... day of .... 18..... .... agrees to fight his .... dog .... pounds weight against .... dog .... pounds weight on the .... day of .... 18.......

The dogs to be weighed at .... o' clock in the .... and fight between .... o' clock in the ....

The deposits to be made as in hereinafter mentioned; to be delivered to .... (who is the final Stakeholder), namely, the first deposit of £........ a side at the making of the match; the second deposit of £........ a side, on the .... of .... at the house of ....; third deposit of £.......... on the .... of .... at the house of ....; fourth deposit of £........ on the .... of .... at the house of ....; fifth deposit of £.......... on the .... of .... at the house of ...., which is the last.

Even now the term 'fighting weight' can be heard around the show ring. This is how the dogs were brought to the pit for action. Stripped down to the bare minimum, iron hard, ribs showing, no fat in sight anywhere. In this condition the dogs were not only fit but, being in a permanent state of hunger, were also more nasty and very 'ready'.

Across the centre of the dog fighting arena was marked a line. This was termed the 'scratch' line. If, after a few rounds of combat, either of the dogs refused to go to the scratch line, it was judged to be the loser. The term 'coming up to scratch' may well have originated from this, meaning of course that if you don't 'come up to scratch' you are not up to the job.

Obviously the people involved with dog fighting were not interested in the well-being of their animals. That is, unless they were good at their job and winning big money for their owners. Very often, dogs which lacked gameness and consequently lost in the pit would be given away or thrown in a sack and left to drown.

With the abolition of bear and bull baiting in 1835, so too should have gone dog fighting. Alas, another 76 years had to go by before it was eventually banned. Thankfully, I was born too late for all this macabre stuff. I suppose for these people it was just a way of life. They knew no different.

As well as the organised dog fighting, other popular 'sports' amongst the men of the day included ratting and badger drawing. The Protection of Animals Act 1911 finally outlawed organised dog fighting and all animal baiting.

Finally, I suppose if any of these barbaric pastimes was to be acceptable, then I would have thought it would have to have been organised rat killing. Again, rules applied, but weren't adhered to as rigidly as for dog fighting. Generally, the weight of the dog determined how many rats were to be killed in a given time. The most famous was a dog called 'Billy' who in 1823 killed 100 rats in 5 minutes, then Jacko who must have been more suited to marathons, having killed 1,000 rats in 1 hour 40 minutes.

Organised rat killing became illegal in 1912. The dogs used were generally the smaller terrier type dogs. Dogs which carried a kill around in their mouths were looked upon as not being very good and were unpopular. Just one snap of the dogs' jaws and the rats were dispatched. The dog should then move on to the next rat.

Phil Drabble, celebrated author and countryman, has often spoken of his first dog. It happened to be a Stafford called Grip. Phil insists that the Stafford is the best ratting dog he has ever seen.

I can recall the tales my father-in-law tells of years gone by when it was nothing out of the ordinary for farmers to send for the dog men and their dogs to eradicate the rat problem. He tells of the many Sunday morning excursions up to the Peak District. Usually the day started off before dawn. My father-in-law, Eric, was the only one with a Stafford. A trip then to pick up Wilf, who had Bull Terriers, and then Sam, who had terriers. At Sam's, large quantities of bacon butties were consumed. Then it was off to wherever they were required.

One story in particular involved an old scrap car which was situated in a field. On arrival, the farmer advised them that he thought the rats were inhabiting the old banger. So off they went across the field. As they approached the car the dogs began squealing in anticipation. They knew something was there. On closer inspection, there didn't seem to be any rats around about at all. Still the dogs wouldn't quieten down. Then they had a brainwave. A trip into the hedge bottom to find a large branch. On arrival back at the car the branch was used as a lever to prise up the back seat. A synchronised one – two – three, and the back seat was up. The farmer was certainly right, for nestling beneath the seat were scores and scores of rats. Rats everywhere, jumping and squeaking, swarming all over the place. Eric tells me at a rough estimate there must have been getting on for 200. As you can imagine, they didn't last long. The dogs had a field day. Eric's Stafford and the other dogs certainly had a morning to remember. The dead rats were piled up into a wheelbarrow and taken into the stack yard for the farmer to dispose of. What a way to spend a Sunday morning. Brilliant!

I say 'brilliant' from a purely personal point of view for I feel that I missed out on this. I would have loved to have been involved in this vermin control. Even people in the neighbourhood would call upon their services if they had the slightest indication that a rat or, even worse, rats were about their houses or gardens. Alas, with the introduction of other methods for vermin control (Rentokil, for example), the dogmen are now very, very rarely called upon, if at all.

So, getting back to the breed's history, with the Protection of Animals Act 1911, practically everything our forefathers participated in was made illegal. Consequently, everything of that ilk was driven underground. So between the years of 1911 and the early 1930s it was realised that, if the Stafford as we know it today was to survive, a new direction was required. In fact, a completely new hobby: the Stafford as a show dog.

In this interim period of just over 20 years there were, obviously, differences of opinion, major arguments and worse. Certain factions could never visualise the Stafford as a show dog. In fact, they regarded the very idea as an insult to the breed. Their breed, the fighting machine, warlike heritage and all. On the other side of the coin was the view that, now that dog fighting was illegal, something else had to be pursued.

Also around this time, dog showing was becoming more popular. What must have been crystal clear during the period from 1911 was the Stafford's temperament. Not just a fighting machine, chained up for most of his life (until he was required for the pit), but a dog so willing to share his better side with his human counterpart. This canine affection, loyalty and general obedience towards their owners must have weighted heavily in the hearts and minds of the pioneers of the breed who wanted so much to take the Stafford away from his barbaric past.

Amongst the very first people trying to shape the Stafford as a show dog were Jack Barnard (first President of the Staffordshire Bull Terrier Club), Maurice Smith (first Chairman) and Joe Dunn (first Hon Secretary). The original Committee Members were Harry Pegg (owner of Fearless Joe and Dee's Pegg, dam of Ch Fearless Red of Bandits), Joe Mallen (owner of Ch Gentleman Jim, Cross Guns Johnson, Good Lad and The Great Bomber), Jack Birch (owner of Vindictive Monty), S W Poole (Lassomine), A Forrest (Dinkie), C Grosvenor (Lady Rose), G Williams (Leston Boy and Brindle Thelma), Miss M Hill and Maurice Smith. This was the very first Committee of the very first club dedicated to the Stafford: the Staffordshire Bull Terrier Club.

These people were responsible for guiding the Stafford in his inception as a show dog. They were rebuffed and challenged all the way, especially by the dog fighting fraternity (who still saw the Stafford as nothing more than a fighting machine) until they finally gained permission from The Kennel Club to have Staffords in an Any Variety Class at an Exemption Show in Cradley Heath in 1935. Again, it wasn't until 1935 that the Stafford was actually named the Staffordshire Bull Terrier and again, after many differences of opinion, it was decided the the County of the dog's origin would be included in the name.

From that first show of 26 entries the first four were:

1   Birch's Monty (later renamed Vindictive Monty)
2   Shaw's Jim (later renamed Jim the Dandy)
3   Pegg's Joe (later renamed Fearless Joe)
4   Mallen's Cross Guns Johnson

It was from Jim the Dandy that the original Breed Standard was derived. Jim the Dandy was 17.5in to the shoulder and 33lb in weight. He was regarded at this time as an ideal specimen of the breed.

This original Standard lasted until 1948, a period of 13 years. In 1948 it was amended again and this one stayed until 1987. In 1987, the Standard was amended only slightly. These Standards are reproduced in full in chapter 2 The Breed Standard.

The Staffordshire Bull Terrier Club was formed in 1935 and this new Club, with The Kennel Club's permission, set the Stafford well on his way to becoming what he still is today: a very popular, top class show dog.

Another landmark for the breed was to be included at Crufts for the first time in 1936. Other clubs formed around this era were:

•   Southern Counties Staffordshire Bull Terrier Club (1937)
•   Northern Counties Staffordshire Bull Terrier Club (1943)
•   North West Counties Staffordshire Bull Terrier Club (1946)

There are now many more, and the majority of them award Challenge Certificates (CCs) to the breed. Staffordshire Bull Terriers were not awarded CCs until 1946, Birmingham Show being the first show to offer CCs for the breed.

At Bath on 4 May 1939 the first Stafford Champions were crowned. The dog was Joe Mallen's Ch Gentleman Jim and the bitch was Joe Dunn's Ch Lady Eve. It seems that the first male Champion of the breed was pied; the current Breed Record Holder for CCs, although 58

1st Lady E

Left: the first bitch champion, Lady Eve.
Right: the first dog champion, Gentleman Jim.

years on and also different in type, is also a brindle and white pied dog. They say history repeats itself, don't they? Who knows, in another 50 years time, our dog Ch Domino Flashy Lad may be held in the same esteem as Ch Gentleman Jim.

Just as a matter of interest, when the breed was first recognised in 1935 Mr H N Beilby looked into and established the Lines and Families of Staffords. He found six main bloodlines. Each was given a letter which would be identified as the stud dog of the line in question. The most successful of these lines is the 'M' line for producing quality specimens and stud dogs.

Our dog Arnie (Ch Domino Flashy Lad) is a direct descendant of the 'M' Line and is the ninth in an unbroken line of champion dogs dating back from 1951.

The Lines are:

- 'J' Line (Fearless Joe)
- 'M' Line (Brindle Mick)
- 'L' Line (Game Lad)
- 'B' Line (Rum Bottle)
- 'R' Line (Ribchester Max)
- 'C' Line (Cinderbank Beauty)

The champion dogs (forming an unbroken lineage) in Arnie's pedigree are:

	Champion	Made up	No of CCs
Fig 1:	Ch Goldwyns Leading Lad	1951	13
Fig 2:	Ch Eastaff Danom	1956	11
Fig 3:	Ch Jolihem Ringmaster	1971	5
Fig 4:	Ch Jokartan Royal Tan	1975	3
Fig 5:	Ch The Malaser Mauler	1984	4
Fig 6:	Ch Lancstaff Sparbu Saga	1988	5
Fig 7:	Ch Rogue Saga	1990	6
	Ch Domino Flashy Lad	1994	28

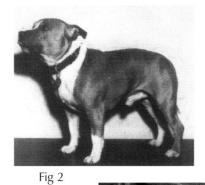

Fig 2

Fig 3

Fig 1

Fig 4

Fig 5

Fig 6

Fig 7

13

CHAPTER 2

TEMPERAMENT

This is the most important feature the Staffordshire Bull Terrier possesses. A Stafford with the 'true' Stafford temperament we often hear about is an absolute joy to own.

Our introduction as a couple to owning Staffords was purely down to this. Although my wife Julie was practically bought up with the breed, our first three years of marriage were dog-free. One of Julie's friends decided to go to America as a child minder. The timing of her leaving England coincided with her parents still being away on holiday. Consequently, there was no one to look after her dog Billy for the week until her parents arrived back from holiday. Obviously, we didn't know at the time, but Billy (Kennel Club name Elvinor Pied Piper, a beautiful red and white pied dog) would become the sire of our two foundation bitches and in turn, as history will show, grandsire to the Breed Record Holder.

The Stafford should be totally trustworthy with children.

It was agreed that we would look after Billy for the said week. I was a bit dubious about the arrangement. All I could think about was their reputation, that they were nasty, would fight anything that moves, and so on. I was very sceptical. How wrong I was! No need to be worried at all. It turned out to be one of the best weeks we had ever had. Julie had been on at me for the past three years that we ought to get our own Stafford. One way or another I always put it off. Eventually, we didn't get one. We got two! We now have six. They are our lives. I cannot imagine living without them.

In that one week, Billy proved to me that Staffords are very intelligent, very affectionate and a real pleasure to have around. They are so affectionate and faithful that it is at times difficult to understand why our forefathers actually bred them for fighting. One thing that was apparent in those days was the willingness of the Stafford to please. This in one sense really annoys

Irresistible!

The Stafford pup should be encouraged to be friendly towards other dogs.

Staffords love children ....

me because the so-called 'macho' men who like to think they've got a fighting machine on the end of the lead do not realise that not only are they discrediting a fabulous breed but the Stafford himself is only doing what he thinks is making his master happy. Whatever the task, if your Stafford thinks he is pleasing you he will be more than happy.

Anyone purchasing a puppy from us is always advised to bring him up firmly so that he always knows who the boss is, but also to encourage an amiable temperament, especially with other dogs.

You may think this will be making your Stafford something of a 'wimp'. You could not be further from the truth. The most placid dog, if needs be, will stand his ground with anything and in no uncertain terms.

I doubt if there is another breed that comes anywhere near the Stafford when it comes to temperament. They make the most fantastic guardians, not only with adults but especially with children. Always remember that, if your Stafford thinks he is making you happy, he is prepared and able to do anything.

With children, Staffords are absolutely without equal. Again, if you think back to what they were originally bred for, their tolerance level is quite unbelievable. Children can at times be very cruel. The child may not comprehend the extent of the cruelty but very often a pencil or finger may be used as a probe and inserted into one or more of the dog's orifices! The Stafford just sort of shrugs his shoulders in a "Well, it's a child – what do you expect?" fashion.

A sight to behold is when a toddler is just about at the crawling and walking via the furniture stage. You will find that the dog tries his utmost to find a quiet spot to get out of the way – possibly to doze off. Very often the dog is followed by the toddler, sometimes even being used as a stabiliser! Being crawled all over and laid on is nothing unusual for the family Stafford to endure. Very often, dog and child both end up asleep together. The dog just takes it in his stride. Quite amazing!

A well known Stafford person once told me that true Stafford temperament is epitomised in the saying, "One minute the pit, next minute the pram." Obviously this must have originated

.... but children and dogs should always be supervised.

years ago in the fighting days of the Stafford but nevertheless it still bears great relevance. The toughest, most boisterous Stafford will become almost 'ballet-dancer like' when tiny tots are around. Just ask anyone who has had children and Staffords.

I am constantly drawn into arguments on this subject, always defending the Stafford, trying to explain to non-Stafford people their temperament and behaviour. I go to great lengths to try to explain what they are like with humans and especially children.

Another well known story which illustrates the relationship between Stafford and child is the one concerning a dog that was owned by Jack Barnard, the first President of the Staffordshire Bull Terrier Club. The dog adored Jack's daughter, who was four years old at the time. Apparently she did not like bedtime and, when the time came, a quick dash into the dog kennel was undertaken. There she'd be found, fussing the dog and vice versa. When anyone went near to collect the child, the dog became so menacing in his role as protector that no one dared to fetch her. In the end the dog was kept inside until the little girl was tucked up in bed. This is just another example of the bond which can be made between a Stafford and any child. One thing to remember is, if you have a Stafford before starting a family, never ignore him when the baby comes along. Too many people fail to realise the unhappiness the dog feels if he is 'shoved out' when the new baby enters the household. This is the time when the dog should be given more fuss than ever. Your Stafford will quickly learn to love the child intensely and guard it with his life if need be.

The Stafford proves to be almost oblivious to pain. This could well be one of the reason why Staffords are so tolerant of children. Stories of our forefathers amputating the limbs of a

Bed mates.

Bulldog whilst it hung on to the head of a bull just to prove its gameness and tenacity to onlookers may be absurd and disgusting but did actually occur. This gameness manifests itself if you are unfortunate enough to witness a Stafford in a real fight. You can do anything: punch him, kick him, even smack him with a shovel! If he is determined he will not let go. You may find yourself observing your Stafford's 'no pain factor' in many different ways.

On one occasion, our first two bitches were playing down on the lawn. Our lawn is very long and allows almost full speed to be built up. In the middle of the lawn we have a well which I have made ornamental. The stonework stands about 2ft 6in high. Anyway, the bitches were thrashing about chasing each other when, about 5–6ft from the well, Bonnie decided to lower down and flip Ginnie up in the air. Ginnie almost did a somersault and hit the stone well at full speed with the back of her head. On witnessing this, my first reaction was, "Oh my God, that's bound to have killed her. She must be dead!" Wrong again. A quick shake of her head and, although she was a little dazed, the rough and tumble carried on.

Another famous old story is the one told by H N Beilby in his book *The Staffordshire Bull Terrier*, written around 1943. This tells of a Stafford who used to cross the street every morning to visit his favourite lamp-post. One particular morning, the dog was hit by a car when half way across the street. Down he went, cracking a couple of ribs and understandably shaken up. A quick shake and he continued over to the lamp-post, where he calmly lifted his leg as normal. This well documented story, as well as my own personal experience, only goes to bear witness that an injury capable of reducing a member of a lesser breed to unconsciousness or even worse does not have any such affect on a Stafford.

The Stafford usually wants to be involved in whatever you may be doing. You might be gardening or doing a spot of DIY in the house and your Stafford will always be at your side, watching and being inquisitive. When my father attempts to make up the fire, his bitch Rosie

18

is always at hand, very often pinching the floor cloth or a piece of coal – always seeking attention and wanting to be in the midst of things.

It is very amusing when people come to our house particularly if they are 'non-dog' people. They sit down on the sofa and it is only a matter of seconds before they have a Stafford on their laps seeking fuss and affection immediately! Our visitors quickly realise how soft Staffords are. They leave the house much wiser with regard to the temperament of Staffordshire Bull Terriers.

Another thing you will notice is just how funny and comical your Stafford can be. My parents' Stafford bitch Rosie is a real live wire. As soon as you walk through the front door, that's it – she's off. We call it the 'wall of death'. She bounces off the chairs, then bounces off the settee. Very often, she runs round the back of your head as you try to take a seat. It is nothing unusual to be sat relaxing when suddenly Rosie will jump up on to the back of the chair, wrap herself around your neck and start licking your face. To read a newspaper is quite impossible. She just won't let you, always trying and often succeeding in jumping up on to your lap.

She also does what we call the water trick. You can fill either her drinking bowl or the full-sized plastic kitchen bowl. It doesn't really matter. As long as one of them is full of water, Rosie isn't bothered. The first thing she'll do is to put one foot into the water. Then she'll have a crafty look round to see if everybody's watching. A gentle pawing of the water is then pursued. After a few seconds, she puts the other foot in and then proceeds to thrash away at the water until the vessel is completely empty. When it is, she picks it up and runs around the garden with it as if to say, "Look at me, look what I've done. Aren't I clever!" It is little things like this which, without doubt, make the Stafford different - always capturing your attention and endearing them to your heart.

Arnie and his mother, Ginnie, are two of a kind. They are always seeking affection. You always have to be stroking them. If you stop, they always bark. Very often, I wish I'd two mechanical arms. As you will find out for yourself, owners of Staffordshire Bull Terriers are so completely satisfied with their dogs that never for one moment could they be persuaded to switch to another breed.

The Stafford is a deeply devoted, fearless, intelligent and unflinchingly loyal friend. As I have said earlier, Staffords are probably the most adaptable dogs going. They can live and be happy almost anywhere. You do not have to adapt to the dog – he will adapt to you. His best asset and most certainly the one thing which will give your Stafford his greatest pleasure will be his role as the family pet. Sharing your home, and more often than not your bed, sharing your fire, being a unique guardian to both yourself and your children. Basically loving to be loved and the centre of attention. The love and affection given to your Stafford will, believe me, be returned immeasurably. There must be thousands of people around the world all with their own little stories about their Staffords – every one unique, very much in keeping with the temperament of the Staffordshire Bull Terrier. Unique!

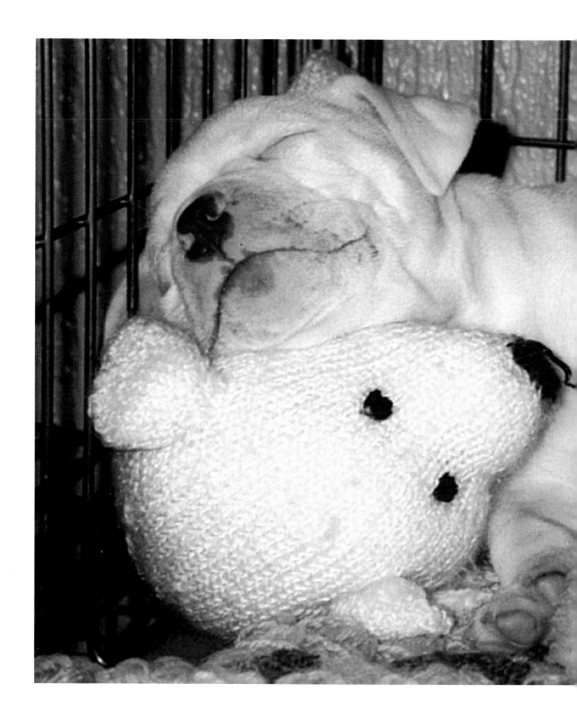

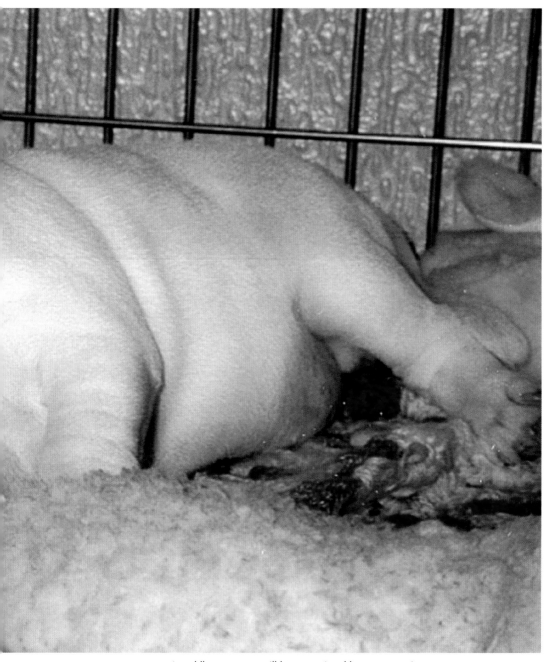

A cuddly toy or two will be appreciated by most puppies.

CHAPTER 3

CHOOSING

If as a complete newcomer to Staffords you find yourself going to look at a litter, very often the one with the nicest markings, the cutest puppy or simply the one that makes the most fuss of you is the automatic choice. Let me assure you that there are a lot more things to consider before you purchase a puppy. After all, you are picking a dog or bitch who will hopefully be your companion and pet for the next 10–15 years.

The first thing you must decide is whether you want a dog or a bitch. I think both make equally fantastic companions. Obviously, if you are buying with a view to future breeding, then it is not a dog you are looking for. Remember, though, that if you own a bitch you will have to endure the oestrus (also known as the 'heat' or

A white bitch puppy.

'season'), which lasts for 3 weeks or so, twice a year. These can prove to be quite messy times. The choice is yours.

If you have never had a Stafford before, it is advisable to ask someone who is experienced in the breed to go along and look at the litter with you. If you do not know anyone involved with Staffords the chances are that you may not know where any litters are. Litters may be advertised in the dog press (*Our Dogs* and *Dog World*, both available from large newsagents), either in the breed notes or the classified section at the back of the paper. Alternatively, a telephone call to The Kennel Club can prove very helpful. Tell them what breed you are interested in and what part of the country you are from. They should then be able to give you names of breeders in your area or the contact numbers for Breed Club Secretaries who may know of current or forthcoming litters. (Please remember that The Kennel Club and the Breed Club Secretaries do not 'recommend' any litters they advise you of, they are simply providing a service.) We often receive telephone calls in this way.

Basically, most reputable breeders of Staffords will be involved with the show side of the breed and are usually known in the show world. Once you have bred a decent litter or litters,

A pied litter.

people don't regard you as a flybynight or someone who's in it for the money. As in every walk of life, there are cowboys and Staffords are no exception. Just be careful and you should be okay. A few pertinent questions on the phone will help you to build a picture of the breeder. You might want to ask:

- What are the sire and dam's temperament like
- Have the puppies been reared indoors or out. Have they been/will they will be socialised. Have they been handled by children and other adults. Are they used to other dogs.

Jeans and trainers get the Stafford pup treatment!

Assessing a puppy for show potential is not easy.

- How many dogs does the breeder own and how many different breeds
- How old is the dam and how many litters has she had previously

It is not vital to take an experienced hand with you but if you are looking for a potential show dog obviously it helps. Having said that, when Arnie's litter was born we had two Championship Show judges come along to look at the litter. At this time the puppies were 6 weeks old. My father-in-law was also a regular visitor and an experienced Stafford owner and

Left: Five weeks old.
Right: Seven weeks old and learning to stand for show.

breeder. This was only our second litter of Staffords. Everyone who had seen the litter was of the same opinion: it was so even at this age that the so-called pick of the litter could not be determined. It was a case of 'close your eyes and point in a certain direction' – in fact, a lottery. Consequently, Arnie was sold at around 7 weeks old. He was given back to us almost 2¹/₂ years later in tragic circumstances.

What I am trying to say is that trying to pick a 6–8-week-old puppy who will turn out to be show-worthy or, even better, a champion is virtually impossible. As a novice, you have as much chance as the next man. In fact, very often the novice pickers end up with the best adults! As I said, the problem is when we 'experienced' people are trying

Ouch!

Although weaned, the pups still relish mother's milk.

Eight weeks old and ready to go to new homes.

to envisage a show quality adult. If you have sought the advice of an experienced breeder, take him or her along to look at the litter and at the pedigree of the puppies. From this he may well be able to inform you of the puppies' ancestry. If the pedigree is accurate, it can give you some idea of how your puppy may turn out when it reaches adulthood. This is where experienced hands can be very helpful. They may well have seen some of the dogs and bitches listed in the pedigree and may have an idea of their size, the main faults and virtues, their colours and, most importantly, their temperaments.

First impressions are important when visiting a breeder: are the puppies being raised in a reasonably clean and stimulating environment? If other dogs are kept, are they in good condition and of sound temperament? You will probably want to visit more than once so that you can see the puppies at different times on different days. If the litter have been sleeping or have tired themselves out by playing just before you arrive, you may be misled into thinking that they are more quiet and docile than they really are! Responsible breeders are more than happy for prospective owners to view the puppies several times, as long as prior notice is given. After all, they want you to be happy with your choice of dog. Let the breeder know what your intentions are - whether the dog is to be a pet or whether you may wish to show him. If he is an experienced exhibitor he may be able to help you with your choice but do bear in mind that no one can give any guarantees as to how a puppy will turn out.

When selecting a puppy with the intention of showing, some people look for specific points. It could be the one with the biggest head, the dome shaped head, the shortest muzzle, the strongest boned, the neatest ears, the best mover, and so on. All of these are very important and everything should be examined before buying.

When Julie and I have either bred a litter or are looking at someone else's litter these are the things we look for: a short muzzle and back, a nice dome-shaped head, dark eyes and small, thin ears. Generally, in puppies aged 6–8 weeks, the ears are hung down Labrador-like. When like this they should hang no further than eye level. Sometimes though at this age the ears have already creased back. Good bone, a straight front, deep brisket and strong hindquarters with a good bend of stifle are also desirable. If the puppy is put together correctly, his movement should be correct. I say 'should be'.

A close look at the puppy's mouth is very important. The top incisors should fit snugly over the lower incisors and these should be level all the way along. The four canines should interlock appropriately. It is generally thought that, if the milk teeth are correctly placed, the second set should also be correct.' This does not always follow, however. We once bred a bitch whose mouth was perfect right up until she was 5 months old. She then became undershot, practically overnight. On the other hand, we have also bred and seen puppies that have been at least 3-4mm overshot. Although this is worrying at the time, they have ended up with perfect mouths. Having spoken to other people in the breed , the assumption must be made that even if a 6–8-week-old puppy is overshot, the lower jaw will eventually catch up, forming the correct scissor bite.

Look for a puppy who enjoys human contact - he will be much easier to train and socialise.

Obviously, at this age it is very difficult to assess temperament. Again, an experienced hand may be able to inform you of temperament of the sire of the litter and even the grandparents.

Puppies raised with children are likely to be outgoing.

The breeder should also be able to enlighten you as to each puppy's individual character and a responsible breeder will wish to place each pup in the most appropriate home. The idea is to match the potential owner, their circumstances and their reason for having a dog to the temperament of the individual pup. Is the dog to be part of a boisterous family, a companion for a more sedate middle-aged owner, a mate for long country walks or strolls round the local parks? Will he live indoors or out, be allowed on the furniture and beds, accompany his owner on all his outings? Is he to be a show dog primarily or purely a pet?

I would look for a friendly, active and lively puppy. It is very easy to see the dam of the litter, for obvious reasons, but sometimes the sire is miles away. Usually a photograph of the sire is all that is available. Check that the dam is friendly towards people (not just her owners) because her attitude can influence the pups enormously.

With these facts in mind, you must make your choice. You should be purchasing a

A predominantly white litter.

healthy, registered and hopefully well-bred puppy. How it turns out at the end of the day is in the lap of the Gods. I say this because many a time we have seen very nice puppies develop into very mediocre adults and vice versa. It is a gamble we all take when selecting our new show dog.

Some breeders register their puppies practically as soon as they are born so by the time they are ready to go the Kennel Club Registration Certificates are there for you to take home along with your new puppy. In our case, we always wait until our puppies have acquired their new owners, who are then given the chance to pick the name of their new puppy. This is just a personal thing as we feel that the people buying the puppies should have the choice of name. The Kennel Club allow a year for puppies to be registered, anyway.

The names of our puppies are always preceded by the word 'Brajulste'. This is our affix and is an combination of our names (Steve and Julie Bradder). Most breeders have an affix. This way, when people are studying a pedigree they can easily identify a certain dog or even a certain line. Affixes are available upon application to The Kennel Club. (At present an affix costs £70 to buy and £20 a year thereafter to maintain it – £17 if by Direct Debit.)

The breeder's affix is always placed (as a prefix) at the front of the dog's name, for instance Brajulste Hell's Bells. However, if we buy a puppy from another breeder, our affix is placed after the name (as a suffix), for instance Brad's Beauty at Brajulste.

A promising black puppy.

Each puppy costs the breeder £12 to register with The Kennel Club. Registration usually takes a couple of weeks (if there are no hitches with the paperwork). When the forms come back, all the puppies are registered in the ownership of the breeder. The new owner then has to transfer the puppy into their ownership. The transfer fee is currently £10. Six weeks free insurance is usually available free of charge to the breeder who registers a litter, which takes effect when they inform the insurance company on the day that the puppy goes to his new home. The insurance company will note the new owner's details for their records.

When you pick up your new puppy you may receive the following, depending on the breeder:

• A signed pedigree form (Champions are usually shown in red ink)
• A diet sheet and details of worming schedule, also some puppy food to tide the puppy

over (hopefully you will have enquired in advance what the breeder is feeding the pups on so that you can purchase the same)
- The Kennel Club Registration Certificate, if it is available
- Insurance document with six weeks free cover
- A signed receipt detailing any conditions of sale

Very promising at fourteen weeks old.

The breeder will probably ask you to let them know in a day or so how the puppy is settling in and, of course, to keep in touch. Get your puppy home as smoothly and quickly as possible. (Do not stop to show him off to friends or relatives!) Remember, he may never have been in a car before so be prepared with newspaper, towels, an empty plastic bag and flannel to clean the pup up in case he is carsick, or worse. It is helpful if someone else can drive while you hold your new addition on the back seat or in a cardboard box. If not, a crate with a snug piece of vetbed will keep the puppy safe and secure during the journey.

If you really need to break your journey, make sure the puppy is wearing a collar and lead, and do not allow him to sniff or walk anywhere where other dogs may have been. Carry him to a clean looking stretch of grass and be very careful that he doesn't slip his collar or try to run off. Once you are home, carry him straight to the area where you want him to do his business and remain patiently with him until he has performed, or you are sure he doesn't yet need to go. If you have another dog, introductions on a neutral piece of territory may be less threatening for the adult. Allow the puppy to explore his new surroundings but be aware that he may squat or circle at a moment's notice, indicating that he is about to urinate or defecate. Quickly but quietly (without panicking him) lift the puppy up and take him out to the garden again. As he performs, give him the command you intend to use, such as "Busy" or "Be clean". Then praise him for being clever and have a short game before taking him inside again.

CHAPTER 4

HEALTH

Vaccination

Puppies are usually vaccinated against four major infectious diseases. It is important that when your puppy is taken for its vaccination injections it is healthy and of the correct age. I say this because all puppies receive some form of protection from their mothers' milk. If the puppy is still being protected by the mother's milk at the time of vaccination, this may interfere with the vaccine, therefore affecting the maximum response to the vaccine.

We always take our puppies at approximately 10 weeks for the first injection. The second injection is administered 2 weeks later. After this second injection, wait for one more week before taking your puppy out and about, especially where a lot of other dogs have been.

After these initial injections, an annual booster is advisable.

The four major diseases I mentioned earlier are:

- Canine Distemper
- Infectious Canine Hepatitis
- Leptospirosis
- Parvovirus

The symptoms for all the above are similar, involving high temperatures, vomiting and dehydration. Fortunately, vaccination in puppyhood against these diseases has practically eradicated them. Kennel Cough may also be protected against and many boarding kennels will require proof of this and the dog's vaccination card before boarding your dog.

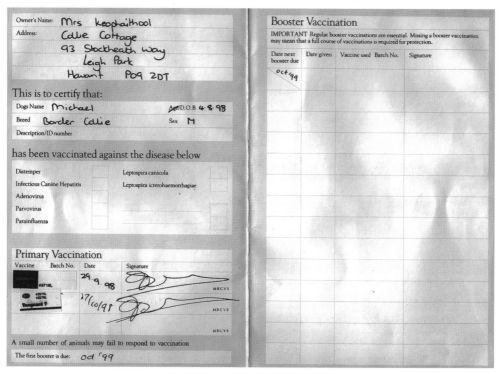

Example of a vaccination card.

Worming

Although I have covered worming of puppies in the Breeding section I feel a bit more information on this is required.

Roundworms

All puppies suffer from roundworms. This group also includes whipworms and hookworms. The most common is the roundworm (Scientific name: *Toxocara canis*). This is like a thin earthworm, usually straw coloured, and a fully grown one can be up to 6in long.

The larvae lie dormant in a bitch and become active again when the bitch is pregnant. The larvae then move and eventually end up in the lungs of unborn puppies via the placenta. Almost all infection is by this method. The larvae can also be passed via the bitch's milk up to 35 days after whelping. So the puppies are actually born with worms.

Infected pups can have breathing and digestive problems (look for 'jelly-like' faeces). Coughing is also a symptom. Fat, pot-bellied puppies are another sign of roundworm infestation.

The experts tell us that 98 per cent of the infection takes place before the puppies are born, with only 2 per cent being passed through the bitch's milk.

The bitch can be re-infected by her pups when she has been licking and cleaning them.

It is a good idea to worm your bitch at the same time as you worm your pups. As I have said, we worm our pups at 4, 6, 8, 10 and 12 weeks of age. Worming your bitch in late pregnancy may help to control the worms in the unborn pups, but consult your vet first.

Tapeworms

Tapeworms are mainly found in adult dogs. Tapeworm control must not be done before 6 months of age.

A whole tapeworm (Scientific name: *Diplidium caninum*) can be 3ft long but usually breaks up into segments and is seen only in the faeces and around the anus. The segments usually look like bits of a broken match or grains of rice.

Tapeworms are never transmitted directly from dog to dog: there is always an intermediate host. This is usually a flea. If one that has the tapeworm larva is swallowed the dog will become infected. The larva develops into a tapeworm and attaches itself to the intestine. It stays there until it is mature and then sheds itself in segments. Tapeworms are easy to get rid of and, as with everything nowadays, a vast selection of treatments is available.

It is best to treat your Stafford (after 6 months of age) four times a year. Not just for tapeworms, but use one of the multi-wormer preparations for both roundworm and tapeworm. It is also wise to keep an eye out for fleas at the same time.

Heatstroke

If you have been fortunate enough not to witness a dog suffering from heatstroke, consider yourself very lucky. You may hear people talking about it and giving advice about how to be careful, especially in hot weather. As the name suggests, heatstroke is more prevalent in the summer months, although too much exercise or over-exertion for a dog that is not accustomed to it can result in the same.

Arnie on one of his walks.

My own experience of heatstroke must have aged me by at least 10 years! On the day in question, I happened to be working nights. I fetched Arnie from Jim's on the Monday afternoon. At this time, Arnie was only 22 months old. It wasn't a particularly hot day, in fact it was late afternoon. Also on this walk came my mate, Mick, and Billy (Elvinor Pied Piper) who, as you know, is Arnie's grandsire and 5 years older.

We decided to go down to Hardwick Hall, road walking on the way there then back through the fields – a round trip of about 5 miles. We arrived at Hardwick after an hour or so – no problems. So to the return trip. We got into the fields about 2 miles from home. At this point both Billy and Arnie were unleashed. There was no vigorous exercise, just basically trotting about around our feet. About a mile from home, Arnie's breathing changed. It became louder and more rapid. A sort of cackling, gasping noise. Mick and I looked at each other and wondered. I was now getting worried. I had never witnessed anything like this before. Also, bear in mind that Billy, Arnie's granddad, was trotting about like a spring lamb.

About half a mile from home, Arnie's breathing was desperate. The noise was horrendous. I was now petrified. Another thing to bear in mind was that, at this time, Arnie was still in the ownership of Jim and Sarah. I was just the handler and exerciser! Imagine how I was feeling at this point. The dog was on death's doorstep and I was responsible!

I picked Arnie up and ran back home as fast as I could. Petrified, stressed out of my mind, I was running on pure fear. The dog's lips were blue, his tongue was blue, even his eye rims were blue. I don't know how I managed to get back home without collapsing myself, but I did.

When I got back home I found the front door locked. A severe hammering on the door got Julie to open it in seconds. She wondered why I had thumped so loudly. When she opened the door and saw Arnie almost dead in my arms and the look of complete fear on my face, she wondered no more. All I could think about was Jim and Sarah. How was I going to tell them that Arnie was dead? We got him straight out on to the backyard and under the tap. Julie turned the tap on full blast whilst I just held the dog with the cold water cascading directly on to the top of his head. I held him there, praying all the time. Both Arnie and I were absolutely soaked. I didn't care! Eventually, after just a few very long moments, the colour began to come back to his lips and tongue. His eyes looked brighter. He was coming round, back from death's door.

When he was completely recovered we let him down on to the lawn where he rubbed up against the fence and once again was running about as if nothing had happened. The look on his face was amazing. It was almost as if he was thinking, "What are you looking at? Is something wrong?" I cannot begin to tell you the relief I was feeling. The dog was going to be all right. I never want to experience that again.

Free-running exercise.

Most dogs will appreciate a change of scenery on their walks.

A fit, well-muscled Stafford.

In the heat of summer, exercise is best left until late evening and early morning.

Also, on a point of note, Arnie at that time had not won a single thing. I could have been responsible for the death of the future Breed Record holder.! Anyway, that's my personal experience with heatstroke and also my own remedy. Maybe it was a little drastic, but it worked.

The main thing to do with a dog with heatstroke is to try to get the temperature down as quickly as possible. When I spoke to a veterinary surgeon about this subject she recommended a slower bringing down of the temperature but, believe me, when you're stressed out of your mind you act accordingly. The normal rectal temperature for a dog is 37-38°C (100-101°F). A dog suffering from heatstroke can have a temperature as high as 43.3°C (110°F). One other story I have heard is of a Stafford suffering from heatstroke being thrown into a canal. It's lucky the canal was nearby.

Ever since my nightmare with Arnie I have been ultra-cautious. Now, even on the coolest of days, I always carry a Jiffy lemon when out walking with any of our Staffords. You know the ones: lemon juice in a plastic lemon-shaped container. The purpose of this is that, at any sign of heavy panting, a quick squirt of this into the mouth soon gets their saliva glands working overtime. You'll find that the dog's not too keen but it means they'll never dry up.

Another thing I always do now is to dip the dog in a water butt sometimes provided at shows. If there is no water butt available, I soak him by other means before travelling back from a show. Travelling to the show is usually no problem as it is more often than not early morning and obviously a lot cooler. Travelling home is a different story. You could be 20–200 miles away from home on a hot day (and it's even hotter in the car) with the prospect of a 3–4 hour journey ahead of you – longer if you hit traffic jams. We took a good friend of ours to Windsor Championship Show a few years ago. Before our return trip, I mentioned to our friend what I intended to do with Arnie before we set off on the return trip. So I dipped Arnie. Pete did not dip his dog. On the way back home, Arnie hardly ever panted. Pete's dog was very hot and bothered. He was lucky we got back home in time. These are just a few of the things we have encountered. You have to be prepared for any eventuality.

Left to his own devices, on a hot day your Stafford would be well out of the sun in a shady, cool area. Didn't someone once write a song, *Mad Dogs and Englishmen go out in the midday sun*? Always remember that your dog doesn't want to be subjected to heat. We put dogs into this situation, so we must also protect them.

Travel

When we travel to the shows, our dogs are always in separate crates in the back of the car. Dog guards can also be used for this purpose; these fit behind the front seat and are secured to the floor and roof of the car. You can also buy dog harnesses which fasten onto the seatbelt fixings of the car. In hot weather, fans can be purchased which run off the cigarette lighter. The ideal is to have air conditioning which ensures that the car remains cool, no matter what the outside temperature may be.

Most show exhibitors have cages designed specifically for their make of car. These usually fit behind the back seats and allow the owners to cage their dog, hang their leads on the cage and to allocate room for their other belongings. When parked, the cage can be padlocked and the tailgate be left up, allowing air to circulate through the car.

Two Bradder Staffords secure in their travel/show cages.

Most cages have removable dividers, allowing more than one dog to be transported. Manufacturers and secondhand cages can be found in the classified section of the dog papers. Cages are also useful to prevent the dog from distracting the driver by pacing, trying to lean out of the window, and so on.

Nail clipping

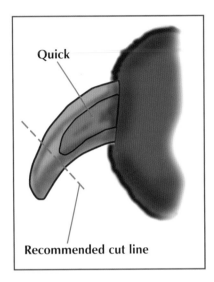

Quick

Recommended cut line

More often than not, regular road walking will keep your Stafford's nails short. Sometimes, though, this is not the case. This is when you must clip the nails or claws yourself. In dogs with white feet, the nails, more often than not, are also white or skin coloured. If this is the case, then nail clipping is relatively easy. The 'quick' of the nail is pink. This part of the nail must not be cut into. If the quick is cut, it will result in the nail bleeding and also pain for the dog.

If you have a Stafford with black feet, then the nails will be black. Therefore, the quick is practically impossible to see, so extreme caution must be exercised. Cut only a little of the nail at a time but at regular intervals to prevent the nail overgrowing.

When I said that it is relatively easy in a dog with white nails, it is, if the dog will allow you anywhere near his or her feet. Let me give you an example. Arnie's outside nails on each of his front feet wear down quite easily with roadwork. However, the middle two on each foot do not seem to wear down in the same way. Every time I've tried to clip them, Arnie has other ideas. As soon as he sees the clippers, that's that. He runs a mile! I've tried holding him in a bear hug while Julie clips them, and vice versa. We've tried sitting on him, lying on him, attracting his attention with a titbit – all to no avail. There's no chance while he's awake. Even when he's asleep, he has one eye open. In the end, I've had to wait until he's in a very deep sleep, in fact dreaming. You know, when their eyes are flickering and whimpering noises are being emitted. This is the only time I can get them and sometimes, believe me, I've had to wait a very long time, quite often into the early hours. What a laugh!

Anal glands

The first time I became aware of anal glands was when one of our bitches started to drag her backside across the floor. Dogs sometimes do this when they have worms. I thought straight away that it couldn't be worms because our dogs are wormed regularly. I took her to our vet, who told me about the blocked anal gland problem that can crop up periodically. He told me that dragging the backside was probably the only form of relief for the dog. He likened it to us having an itch in the same place, the only difference being that we can relieve it with our finger nails! These glands are situated just inside the anus. If you visualise a clock face, they are positioned at about 4 o' clock and 8 o' clock.

Having watched the vet empty the glands the first time, I thought that I would have a go myself next time. This I did, and I have been doing so ever since. Just hold your Stafford's tail up with one hand. Then, with the thumb and forefinger of your other hand, gently but firmly squeeze the anus together. It has to be squeezed out about an inch from the opening. This is where the glands are and ensures that the y are being squeezed.

All that is squeezed out is brown, very smelly liquid which would otherwise be retained by these glands. After a period of time (when the dog starts dragging), the glands are ready for clearing out. A word of warning: it is wise to use a paper towel or some sort of cloth when doing this. If you don't, do it outside where the liquid can be washed away. More importantly, keep your head out of the way. The liquid is vile. It is not very pleasant when it splats up into your face. Believe me – I speak from experience!

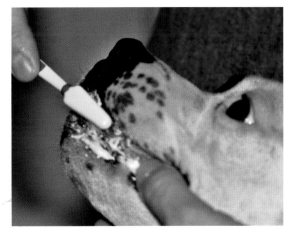

Above: Cleaning Arnie's teeth.
Below: Enjoying a Nylabone.

Teeth cleaning

This part of owning a Stafford is very easy. Basically, the correct diet and the avoidance of sweet things will preserve the life of your dog's teeth. Different types of chews and treats are also available I like to use Nylabone products as they are specifically designed to aid the health of dogs teeth and gums. Big beef knuckle bones are also ideal for this.

As your Stafford gets older some build-up of plaque will be inevitable. If it gets too bad and is causing the dog any distress or bad breath you can have the teeth scraped and cleaned by your vet. We've had one of ours done like this. The dog has to be under anaesthetic for this.

Special 'doggy' toothpaste and

toothbrushes can also be purchased. The toothpaste is flavoured and means that the dog will try to lick away at it whilst you whisk the toothbrush round his mouth. If you let the dog lick the toothbrush afterwards, he will realise it is not such a bad experience.

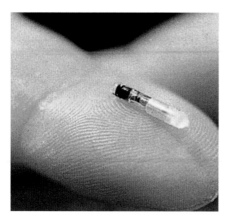

A microchip.

Microchipping

As well as insurance, there are basically two ways to ensure that your Stafford can never lose his or her identity. One is tattooing and the other one, about which I know more, is indentichipping or microchipping.

Arnie was microchipped in 1996. It is a very simple procedure which I think can be likened to ear piercing. I say this from the point of view of administering it. The chip, which is about the size of a piece of matchstick approximately 6mm long, is placed into an injector gun. The gun is then placed at the back of the dog's neck or shoulder area. Then the gun is triggered. The dog doesn't even know it's gone in. When it's been put in, the chip can be scanned. It's like scanning the bar codes on goods at the checkout of your local supermarket.

Each chip has a personal identification number which, when scanned, comes up on an electronic readout. Once you have had your Stafford chipped, the identification number is logged into a database. The database is administered by The Kennel Club, using the name 'Petlog'. Access to this information is available to the RSPCA, the WoodGreen Animal Shelter and other authorised agencies for 24 hours a day.

Arnie and Ginnie..

Care of the elderly dog

Ageing is a natural process, with the obvious slowing down of your once boisterous Stafford. More frequent visits to the vet may be necessary and more 'accidents' in the home will probably take place. Be aware that if you have insurance for your dog, some companies may not insure a dog aged 8 or over, or only for accidental injury (not illness). Some companies will not accept a new pet onto their books if he is 8 or over, so it pays to shop around.

Euthanasia

This is a heartbreaking but important part of the ownership of any animal. From a personal point of view, I wish it could be introduced for humans as well as animals. I'm sure most of us have known friends or relatives who have suffered the effects of terminal cancer. Witnessing this is quite unbearable. At least with animals we have a choice. My in-laws and parents, being dog-owners for longer than us, have had several dogs put to sleep; so far Julie and I have only had to have one Stafford put down. The following is her story.

Ginnie.

Panama Princess (Ginnie), Arnie's dam, was only eight years old. Everything seemed fine until one Monday when Ginnie would not eat her food. She was also lying down more than usual and had vomited some bile. We took her straight to the vet.

Having listened to her symptoms he gave her a painkilling steroid injection and asked us to return the following day which we did but there was no improvement in her condition. This time she was given two injections and the vet said that if there was still no improvement he would take a blood sample the next day. By this time she was practically having to be carried everywhere - all her strength had gone and we knew something was drastically wrong with her. The blood sample was taken and sent away, with the results due back the next day (Thursday). We returned with Ginnie before the results had been received. Ginnie was now so ill that the vet decided to open her up to see if he could find anything (such as a blockage). As soon as she was under the vet noticed a lump in her stomach. On further inspection this turned out to be peritonitis. This was bad enough but worse was to come. Ginnie was also suffering from cancer of the pancreatic gland. The results of the blood test came back whilst she was under anaesthetic. They revealed cancer of the pancreas but the vet had already found it. He phoned up to ask if we wanted to have Ginnie put to sleep whilst she was still under the anaesthetic. I asked him if there was any chance. He said no and that if she was allowed to come round she would probably last for 48 hours at the most and would be in sheer agony. After hearing this we had no choice.

The constitution of a Stafford is such that even if they are suffering from an illness such as cancer, they only take ill (and I mean really ill) days before they die. In our case, with Ginnie, she was offish on Monday and on Thursday she was put to sleep to save further suffering, a fighter right to the end, so typical of this best of all breeds. God bless you.

CHAPTER 5

DIET AND EXERCISE

Diet

This element of Staffordshire Bull Terrier ownership now could not be easier. Gone are the days when trips to the local abattoir to fetch raw tripe were common. The home-made recipes also seem to have died out although some people, especially the traditionalists, still prefer these.

A stainless steel water bowl will age well and will not break if accidentally dropped. Ideally, water should be changed twice daily, especially in summer, and after the dog has returned from heavy exercise. Food bowls should be picked up as soon as the dog has finished his meal and washed daily. Combined food/water bowls are impractical and most are too tiny to be of any use.

To begin with, it is helpful to your pup to continue to feed him on the food he received whilst at the breeder's - this will avoid tummy upsets in the potentially early stressful days when your new pup is settling

Raised food and water bowls on sale at a show.

in. If you wish to feed a different brand, do so slowly by gradually adding it to the original food, whilst decreasing the amount of original food that you feed. If you have a fussy eater, try warming the food first or adding tripe, tinned fish or cheese. It is unnecessary to supplement dry food diets - in fact it can do more harm than good, especially to a growing pup. However, it does not hurt an older dog to be given a little cod liver oil in winter, to help his joints. Garlic is also useful in the fight against fleas and is thought to be good for the heart.

There are so many different manufacturers of dog foods today that the choice is fantastic. There are also many dog food outlets now, including pet superstores. Manufacturers also have stands at breed shows, especially the All Breed Championship Shows. If you require help or advice about feeding, never be afraid to ask. The people on these stands are very knowledgeable about their products and they often have samples for your dog to try.

Our own preference is for Pedigree Petfoods. Their range covers everything from puppies through to adulthood. All the other brands also offer this but, as I said, Pedigree is our preference. There are so many different flavours. One 400g tin plus a couple of handfuls of Pedigree mixer is sufficient for your Stafford on a daily basis. Everything your dog needs is in there: the necessary proteins, carbohydrates, fats, calcium and phosphorus. Out of the many flavours available, ours particularly enjoy Pedigree Chum with Chicken and Sunflower Oil. Whatever the flavour, a breakdown of the ingredients and nutritional value is written on the can. For instance:

Sunflower Oil Enhances the condition of your dog's coat and skin so that it shines with health.
Calcium and Phosphorus Correctly balanced for strong, healthy teeth and bones.
Protein For muscle building, body maintenance and repair.

Stainless steel bowls are easy to clean and virtually indestructible.

Carbohydrates and Fats Carefully controlled to meet your dog's energy requirements.

Not only are the ingredients and reasons for them supplied, there is also a feeding guide. You really can't go wrong. Just find a food that your Stafford likes, remembering that a supply of fresh water is vital at all times. It is also important never to over-indulge, although if the feeding guides are followed over-indulgence is impossible.

Some people prefer to use dry food. This also is nutritionally balanced with your dog's health in mind so that everything is in there. As the name suggests, this food is dry, so fresh water must be readily available. Some people prefer to soak the food before feeding, either to release the juices in the food or to prevent the food expanding within the dog's stomach.

Once you have found a food that is acceptable to your Stafford you must then decide when it is most convenient for you to feed him. We (that is Julie, for she is in charge of feeding in our house) feed only once a day. This takes place at 6.00–7.00 pm. You may find another time more convenient, or you may wish to split your dog's meal into two and then feed morning and evening. Having more than one Stafford, we always feed them separately to avoid fights over food. When you feed more than one together, even if they have their own bowls, one will be more greedy than the other, so consequently the greedier one will finish first. He or she will then go over to finish the other's meal. At this point, the trouble begins. A Stafford will defend its food, believe me! If you only have one, obviously this situation will not arise.

It is natural for any dog to enjoy chewing a bone and it is also very beneficial in keeping the teeth clean. Marrow bones are usually safe to give because they cannot easily be broken down. Always avoid pork or chicken bones as they splinter and can quite easily get stuck in your Stafford's throat, or digestive tract, causing severe problems. Even roast bones from the pet shop can cause a problem if the dog is allowed to gnaw at the bone for too long. If your dog has a blockage he will struggle to defecate, may vomit up bile and generally be very off-colour. Veterinary assistance should be sought without delay. The dog may require an enema(s), or even an operation, to remove the blockage.

Some people advocate variety in a dog's diet but here we err on the side of caution. Some Staffords seem to appreciate a change now and again, but not all. Some of ours have reacted with digestive upsets. My advice on this is that, if your Stafford is happy with his diet, then leave it. If you feel that variety is necessary, the easiest way is to offer your dog any of the other flavours available within each brand.

To be honest, we do not advocate feeding between meals or giving titbits, although many biscuits and treats are available. Treats can be very useful when you are training your Stafford, especially for the show ring, or when used as a reward for doing something well.

The best way to keep an eye on your Stafford's feeding habits and general health is to use your own eyes. If your dog appears happy and alert, bright eyed, in good coat and neither overweight nor underweight he will be in good health and receiving all the benefits of a properly balanced diet. If this is the case, you must be doing right. Together with your Stafford, you will learn and eventually find the right formula.

Before: Rosie enjoying my parents' lawn.

If problems arise, seek the advice of your vet.

Exercise

As with probably everything to do with Staffordshire Bull Terriers, there are many differing views on this subject. All I will endeavour to do is to give you my views and how I exercise ours.

Firstly, we are very fortunate in that we have a very big garden which is mainly lawned. This is extremely handy when you don't happen to feel like going out on a trek. If you are a keen gardener (I am not, I hasten to add) then letting a Stafford loose on your prize lawn is not a wise thing to do. Also, if you have nicely organised flower beds, do not expect them to remain so if you are going to allow your Stafford anywhere near them. My mother and father can certainly vouch for this. Pre-Stafford, they possessed a sort of mini-show garden. Beautifully maintained lawn, attractive flower beds, planters,

After: my parents' garden now. Concrete city!

45

Puppies on the prowl.

ornamental wheelbarrows awash with colour. They then had a lovely Stafford bitch puppy from us. Rosie, as she is affectionately known, was a natural born digger, as I think most of them are if left unattended! Needless to say, now, almost 18 months later, 75 per cent of my parents' garden has been paved. This is just one example of which I have personal knowledge. I'm sure there are thousands more. I know I've strayed off the subject somewhat but I think it is vital that, if you are owning a Stafford for the very first time, you are made aware of the fact that they do like soil and they do like to dig.

Now back to the exercise. In general, a Stafford will go and go all day, if permitted. Having said that, when you first arrive home with your new puppy you can completely forget about exercise. Aside from going taking your puppy out to socialise it, you can allow it the freedom of your garden or hard area for at least 6–8 months. This will allow everything to grow properly in its own time. Bones, muscles and joints, etc. Some people say even longer, but the 6–8 months may be used as a minimum time.

Also with puppies I think it is important to a

Rosie indulges her love of digging.

Steve and Arnie.

certain degree just to let them do what they want to do. If they want to sleep or rest, that's fine. If they want to run around and play, this also is no problem.

Staffords, as has been frequently noted, are very adaptable dogs. They are equally at home if you live in the country or in an inner city area.

As you 'grow up' with your Stafford, you will become increasingly aware of his own particular needs with regard to exercise. Maybe you'll find that one mile's road walking combined with some loose running in the fields is adequate. Maybe more, maybe less. Alternatively, you may find yourself with no choice but to do one or the other. Everything is dependent on where you

A picture of health.

be barking or growling or even silly enough to strike the first blow, you Stafford will not, I assure you, finish second.

When I am out with any of ours, I generally take no more than two any one time. I am always aware and ready for any impending danger, particularly if one is running loose. I mostly go on the same route which is about a five-mile round trip. This involves about a 50/50 split – 50 per cent walking on the lead and the other half running loose in fields and lanes.

When I say 'always be ready for the unexpected', I can tell you of one experience which was unpleasant to say the least. On this particular occasion I was out with one of our young bitches. We were on the disused railway, which is about 2 miles away from our house. She had probably been off the lead for about an hour or so, with no problems. We came to a point on the old railway where it veered off to my right, a sort of blind bend. As we approached it, our Bella was about 20 metres away from me. The next thing I saw coming from the other side of the blind bend was another dog. To my horror, the other dog was another Stafford. I shouted and called her name, all to no avail. There was only one thing on her

happen to live. As I said earlier, your Stafford will adapt, wherever you live.

If you find yourself with access to open fields or for that matter any sort of free-running area, the temptation to unleash your Stafford will become irresistible. In this circumstance, I would advise extreme caution. Always make sure that you can see for quite a considerable distance around you. Never release him if you can see someone else out with a dog. I say this because until you get to know your Stafford there is no guarantee that your newly unleashed charge will automatically come back to you on command, particularly if another dog has been spotted. Staffords do not generally start fights but if a Stafford finds himself confronted by another dog who happens to

Above: Roadwalking two Staffords.
Below: Off-lead exercise - be careful!

The author with his best friends.

mind. By this time, the owner of the other dog was also doing the same as me – again to no avail.

Before either of us had time to reach them, there had been a snarl by one or the other of them, at which point the dog proceeded to ram my bitch's head into the old railway lines by means of a good grip on her throat. There were a few very frightening moments, as the dog was determined not to let go. Eventually, after a lot of shouting and yelling from both of us (we actually had to twist the dog's collar and choke him off) he decided to let go. As it turned out, I knew the other owner. He is the landlord of our local pub. We share a laugh about it now but at the time it was very frightening. It could have been so much worse.

Please do not think I am trying to discourage you from free-running your Stafford, but I cannot over-emphasise the importance of being aware when you are out with your dog. Always be one step ahead. Think for him, especially when he is loose. I can speak from experience about that time on the old railway. I hope that with care and common sense you never have to experience the same. **Please be very, very careful. It is of vital importance.**

To sum up, basically there are no hard and fast rules regarding exercising your Stafford. Just find a time and a distance which suits both of you. It may be that it's only 10 minutes a day, it could be 2–3 hours a day. Throwing a ball or favourite toy will help to keep your dog fit (and his attention on you), especially if time is limited. Just be careful that he can't swallow the ball or toy, which should ideally be larger than the entrance to the throat. In the summer months it is wiser to exercise dogs at the beginning and end of the day, to avoid overheating.

Finally, as your Stafford approaches old age (which could be anything from eight years of age onwards), you will probably notice him start to slow down. Very often you will see older Staffords being exercised off the lead. This is because, more often than not, the older dog cannot be bothered to fight or run off anymore - not because he is more obedient! As mentioned earlier, Staffords are very adaptable and will let you know when it is time to ease back a bit. Until they do, I allow mine to take as much exercise as they wish. Keeping your Stafford fit will make his later years more pleasurable and, hopefully, help to lengthen his lifespan.

CHAPTER 6

BASIC TRAINING, HANDLING AND SOCIALISATION

'Hello'

When you arrive home with your newly-acquired Stafford you will have to decide how you will begin to train him. Everyone's methods are different, so again all I will tell you about is how we train ours. Hopefully, we all end up with a well trained, obedient dog.

The first thing to remember is that, if you have bought a puppy in, its first night with you is also its first night away from its litter-mates. It will be in totally different surroundings to those to which it has become accustomed: different smells, different sights, different people and, more importantly, no litter-mates. For the first few nights it will be very lonely so be ready for several noisy nights. After these initial times the puppy should settle down. Some people say that a cuddly toy or something similar should be put with the puppy in its sleeping quarters, even a ticking clock – anything to keep it company and for it to snuggle up to.

Now you need to decide where your new puppy is going to sleep. On this point, we always advocate the use of cages. Some people are very much against these but, if you introduce your new puppy to a cage straight away, it very quickly becomes its home, its own little house. To begin with, you can feed your pup in the cage so that he looks forward to going in there and sees it as a positive experience. Then the pup can be given a nice titbit or safe chew article, together with a soft toy and something carrying your scent (perhaps an old jumper) to keep him company whilst the door is closed for a short period. Build this up until the pup is quite happy to settle down and await your return. A radio left on low may also be a comfort. When you are at home there is obviously no need for the cage as you can keep your eye on the pup. On the other hand, if you are out at work or nip out shopping or are out for

A Nylabone fold away pet carrier complete with food and water bowls.

any reason, the damage an unrestrained Stafford pup can do is immense.

Let me give you an example. When we had our first two bitches, nobody told us about cages. We had just had a brand new conservatory built onto the back of our house. Ideal, we thought, to keep our new puppies in. Ideal indeed! Within a couple of months, it was practically wrecked: the door, the skirting boards, the floor boards – in fact, the lot!

The crate can be made cosy by adding a soft blanket or duvet.

When you are with Staffords, you wouldn't think butter would melt in their mouths. When they are left unattended, they can and do cause havoc. Be warned! So, from a cage point of view, when you are out, they are in them – when you are in they are not. However, remember to build up the time that your pup spends in his cage very gradually and never leave him for longer than a couple of hours when he is an adult and, of course, for even shorter periods whilst he is a puppy. Never leave a collar on a dog in a crate as accidents can all too easily happen.

The easiest way to house train your puppy is to get him into a routine. Puppies need to go outside straight after waking, after playing, after being fed and, on average, every hour or so. At this age they have very small bladders and cannot be expected to 'hold on'. The signs of a pup needing to 'go' include suddenly walking with his nose to the ground, an earnest expression, or circling. When this happens you only have a matter of seconds to scoop the puppy up and take him outside. Stay with the pup while he does his business, so that you know he has 'been' and so you can praise him for being good. If you shut the pup outside he may fret to come in and will then do his business inside - not what you want at all!

"When you are with Staffords, you wouldn't think butter would melt in their mouths."

This could have been avoided if the puppy had been IN his crate!

Another helpful tip is to keep an amount of newspaper down at all times when toilet training a new puppy. Gradually keep moving this towards an outside door until eventually your puppy will be going outside to do its business. There is a well-known saying that dogs will not dirty where they sleep. As a rule, this is true, but it also depends on the size of the pup's sleeping quarters. This is why having his own crate can also assist in your pup's house training. If you pop the pup in to sleep or when you cannot supervise him, he is less likely to mess his quarters. Do be fair, though, and only use it for short periods. The crate should never be an excuse to leave a dog for hours on end.

It also helps if you use a command to accompany the procedure. We always say, "Down the garden!" or "Tiddles!" You may find yourself using even sillier words, but it does help. In this way you can ensure that your dog has emptied before he goes in the car, into the show ring and any other time when you do not want a 'mistake'! You will inevitably encounter mishaps along the way but hopefully, as your puppy matures, the mishaps should lessen and finally disappear. Never punish the pup for making a mistake indoors or the process will

The author's litters spend time both inside and out, giving them a wide range of experiences.

inevitably become a fearful and protracted one. Blame yourself for not being there in time to take the pup outside.

There are not many who keep their Staffords in kennels all the time. Basically, Staffords are not kennel dogs. They love human companionship too much for that. We have kennels and runs out the back and these are used when we are out at work or for long periods for any other reason. When we are home the house is quickly Stafford-ridden.

It is most important to socialise your puppy early. Hopefully, your puppy will have been socialised to a certain degree by the breeders. We always have our puppies in and around the house from the age of about 4 weeks. This way they get used to the other dogs and different people coming and going. They also get used to all the normal household sounds such as the telephone, doorbell, washing machine, hoover and so on. At this age they take things in their stride and so this is just the time to keep pushing their personal development by allowing them to have new experiences and encounters which will broaden their world. Puppies that have not been socialised at all always seem to be somewhat reserved and stand-offish. Of course you can try to rectify this when the puppy is in your ownership but the damage may already have been done.

It is important to continue the socialisation training once you have bought your pup home. It is an easy matter to take the pup round the local shopping precinct, to the railway station, past the school and on the bus with you. Most people love puppies and will stop to say hello and pet the dog. Always remember to carry a plastic bag to clean up after your dog - you can be fined if you don't. It is also unfair to other pedestrians and park users - dog owners have lost the use of public facilities before through the selfish actions of a few.

The bond between a Stafford and his owner is almost second nature. However, when socialising with other dogs, a little extra care has to be taken. For this reason, it is a good idea to attend training classes. These are held more or less every week. They are run by different clubs up and down the country. (Contact The Kennel Club or look in the dog press for details of your local registered societies.) Training classes basically fall into two categories: ringcraft classes (training for the show ring) and obedience classes (for obedience training).

In the main, Staffords are not generally trained in the field of obedience, mainly because of their intolerance towards other dogs. However, we have seen some very good videos, particularly from Australia/New Zealand, of Staffords participating in Obedience events with very great success. It is amazing to see loose Staffords not bothering at all with each other.

Ringcraft classes, although mainly used as training for the show ring, can be very beneficial for socialising your Stafford. It gets them used to being with and near other dogs. We go to an

A Stafford pup at a Ringcraft class.

All-Breed canine society training class. In this our Stafford sees for the first time tiny Toy breeds right up to some of the massive breeds from the Working or Hound Groups. The trainers will give advice on how to handle your dog, especially if you have a troublesome, over-boisterous or over-exuberant Stafford. Attendance at class will also give you some idea how your dog will react when he see other dogs - this will be very useful when you are out in the community.

Don't forget though that socialisation doesn't end with your dog. You can also enjoy a good night out, having a drink or two, and engaging in 'doggy talk with people from all different kinds of breeds. Good friendships can be forged just by attending these training and social nights.

CHAPTER 7

STAFFORDSHIRE BULL TERRIER
BREED STANDARDS

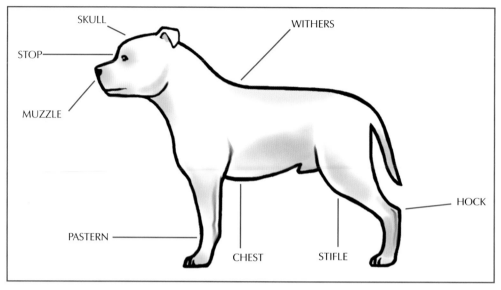

Points of the dog.

The first Breed Standard for the Staffordshire Bull Terrier was published in 1935. There were revised editions in 1948 and 1987.

Breed Standard 1935

General Appearance The Staffordshire Bull Terrier is a smooth coated dog, standing about 15–18in high at the shoulder. He should give the impression of great strength for size and, although muscular, should be active and agile.

Ch. Midnight Gift *(Champion in 1939)*

Head Short, deep through, broad skull, very pronounced cheek muscles, distinct stop, short foreface, mouth level.

Ears Rose, half prick and prick, these three to be preferred, full drop to be penalised.

Eyes Dark

Neck Should be muscular and rather short.

Body Short back, deep brisket, light in loins with forelegs set rather wide apart to permit chest development.

Front Legs Straight, feet well padded, to turn out a little and showing no weakness at pasterns.

Hind Legs Hindquarters well muscled, let down at hocks like a terrier.

Coat Short, smooth and close to skin.

Tail The tail should be of medium length tapering to a point and carried rather low. It should not curl much and may be compared with an old-fashioned pump handle.

Weight Dogs: 28–30lb; Bitches: 4lb less.

Colour May be any shade of brindle, black, white, fawn or red or any of these colours with white. Black and tan and Liver not to be encouraged.

Faults To Be Penalised Dudley nose, light or pink eye rims, tail too long or badly curled, badly undershot or overshot mouths.

Scale of points 1935

General appearance, coat and condition 15
Head 30
Neck 10
Body 25
Legs and feet 15
Tail 5
Total 100

Breed Standard 1948

Characteristics From the past history of the Staffordshire Bull Terrier, the modern dog draws his character of indomitable courage, high intelligence and tenacity. This, coupled with his affection for his friends, and children in particular, his off duty quietness and trustworthy stability, makes him the foremost all purpose dog.

General Appearance The Staffordshire Bull Terrier is a smooth coated dog. He should be of great strength for his size and, although muscular, should be active and agile.

Head and Skull Short, deep through, broad skull, very pronounced cheek muscles, distinct stop, short foreface, black nose.

Eyes Dark preferable but may bear some relation to coat colour. Round of medium size and set to look straight ahead.

Ch. Fearless Red of Bandits
(Champion in 1948)

Ears Rose or half prick and not large. Full drop or prick to be penalised.

Mouth The mouth should be level, ie the incisors of the bottom jaw should fit closely inside the incisors of the top jaw and the lips should be tight and clean. The badly undershot or overshot mouth to be heavily penalised.

Neck Muscular, rather short, clean in outline and gradually widening towards the shoulders.

Forequarters Legs straight and well boned, set rather wide apart, without looseness at the shoulders and showing no weakness at the pasterns, from which point the feet turn out a little.

Body The body should be close coupled, with a level topline, wide front, deep brisket, well sprung ribs and rather light in loins.

Hindquarters The hindquarters should be well muscled, hocks let down with stifles well bent. Legs should be parallel when viewed from behind.

Feet The feet should be well padded, strong and of medium size.

Tail The tail should be of medium length, low set, tapering to a point and carried rather low. It should not curl and may be likened to an old-fashioned pump handle.

Coat Smooth, short and close to the skin.

Colour Red, fawn, white, black or blue or any of these colours with white. Any shade of brindle or any shade of brindle with white. Black and tan or liver colour not to be encouraged.

Weight and Size Weight: dogs 28–38lb; bitches 24–34lb.
Height: 14–16in at the shoulder, these heights being related to weight.

Faults *To be penalised in accordance with the severity of the fault:* Light eyes or pink eye rims. Tails too long or badly curled. Non-conformation to the limits of weight or height. Full drop or prick ears. Undershot or overshot mouths.

The following points should debar a dog from winning any prize: Pink (Dudley) nose. Badly undershot or overshot mouth. Badly undershot, where the lower jaw protrudes to such an extent that the upper incisors do not touch those of the lower jaw.

Note Male animals should have two apparently normal testicles fully descended into the scrotum.

Ch Rogue Saga.

Scale of Points 1948

General appearance, coat and condition	10
Head	25
Neck	10
Body	25
Legs and feet	15
Tail	5
General movement and balance	10
Total	100

Breed Standard (Current)

Reproduced by kind permission of The Kennel Club

In 1987 The Kennel Club called for changes in the wording of the Breed Standard. It is practically identical to the 1948 one, however, because The Kennel Club indicated that it did not wish to alter the definition itself, only the wording.

Breed clubs around the country attempted to discuss the matter in open forums. These were not very successful, as the topic of the debate always ended up being the height and weight clause. By the way, this argument about the correct height corresponding to the correct weight went on in the early 1930s, still goes on today and probably will still be going on in another 60 years!

It is reckoned that for every half inch in height $2^1/2$lb in weight should be the equivalent gain. The following tables illustrate this.

Dogs	**Bitches**
14in 28lb	14in 24lb
$14^1/2$in . . . .$30^1/2$lb	$14^1/2$in . . . .$26^1/2$lb
15in 33lb	15in 29lb
$15^1/2$in . . . .$35^1/2$lb	$15^1/2$in . . . .$31^1/2$lb
16in 38lb	16in 34lb

Although these tables only show the weights and heights as called for in the Standard, very often exhibits that are, in the main, far taller than the Standard calls for are seen entered in shows. It goes without saying that if a dog is 18in at the withers, its relative weight, if the table is used, should be 48lb (4lb less if this relates to a bitch). You don't have to be Albert Einstein to discover that this is 2in taller and 10lb heavier than the Standard requires.

Don't get me wrong. Staffords come in all shapes and sizes and Julie and I love them all. I am talking from a purely 'show' point of view.

So, getting back to 1987. Some improvements were made but unfortunately some terms such as 'light in the loins' were omitted.

This is the latest Standard and, obviously, the most important because it is the one in use today:

General Appearance Smooth-coated, well balanced, of great strength for his size. Muscular, active and agile.

Characteristics Traditionally of indomitable courage and tenacity. Highly intelligent and affectionate especially with children.

Temperament Bold, fearless and totally reliable.

Head and Skull Short, deep through with broad skull. Very pronounced cheek muscles, distinct stop, short foreface, nose black.

Eyes Dark preferred but may bear some relation to coat colour. Round, of medium size, and set to look straight ahead. Eye rims dark.

Ears Rose or half pricked, not large or heavy. Full, drop or pricked ears highly undesirable.

Mouth Lips tight and clean. Jaws strong, teeth large, with a perfect, regular and complete scissor bite, ie upper teeth closely overlapping lower teeth and set square to the jaws.

Neck Muscular, rather short, clean in outline gradually widening towards shoulders.

Forequarters Legs straight and well boned, set rather wide apart, showing no weakness at the pasterns, from which point feet turn out a little. Shoulders well laid back with no looseness at elbow.

Body Close-coupled, with level topline, wide front, deep brisket, well sprung ribs; muscular and well defined.

Hindquarters Well muscled, hocks well let down with stifles well bent. Legs parallel when viewed from behind.

Feet Well padded, strong and of medium size. Nails black in solid coloured dogs.

Tail Medium length, low-set, tapering to a point and carried rather low. Should not curl much and may be likened to an old-fashioned pump handle.

Gait/Movement Free, powerful and agile with economy of effort. Legs moving parallel when viewed from front or rear. Discernible drive from hindlegs.

Coat Smooth, short and close.

Colour Red, fawn, white, black or blue, or any one of these colours with white. Any shade of brindle or any shade of brindle with white. Black and tan or liver colour highly undesirable.

Size Desirable height at withers 35.5–40.5cm (14–16in), these heights being related to the weights. Weight: Dogs 12.7–17kg (28–38lb); Bitches 11–15.4kg (24–34lb).

Faults Any departure from the foregoing points should be considered a fault and the seriousness with which the fault should be regarded should be in exact proportion to its degree.

Note Male animals should have two apparently normal testicles fully descended into the scrotum.

My Interpretation of the Breed Standards

As I said earlier, the 1948 and 1987 Standards are virtually the same. So for almost 50 years neither people in the breed nor The Kennel Club have felt that a dramatic change in the Standard has been required.

The major change from the original Standard is the height reduction. This argument is still rife today. I suppose it always will be.

Just try to visualise an 18in dog weighing 38lb. Then visualise a 16in dog weighing the same. It is obvious that the latter of the two, the modern show type, is bound to be a smaller, more compact, in fact a more balanced specimen than the one from yesteryear.

Before I go on and try to interpret the Standard as I see it, let me just say that everyone is entitled to his opinion and let me also assure you that different people see and interpret the Standard in very different ways. I suppose it's part of the attraction of showing a Stafford. The uncertainty of it all probably keeps people going, show after show.

General Appearance, Characteristics and Temperament

The first three points of the Standard generally need no explanation. In particular, the second and third, Characteristics and Temperament respectively. The first, General Appearance, contains the term 'well balanced'. This is very important; it is no use having a dog with a first class head if the rest doesn't balance out at the back of it.

Head and Skull

This is probably the most important physical feature. Basically, the Stafford is a head breed. No head, no Stafford! This is what gives so many breeds their 'breed type'. I always think that a well balanced head can be split up into thirds. From the tip of the nose to the stop one third (this being the muzzle or foreface), and from the stop to the occiput (back of the skull) making up the other two thirds. This, coupled with all the other requirements in this section of the Standard, is what gives the Stafford a classic head shape.

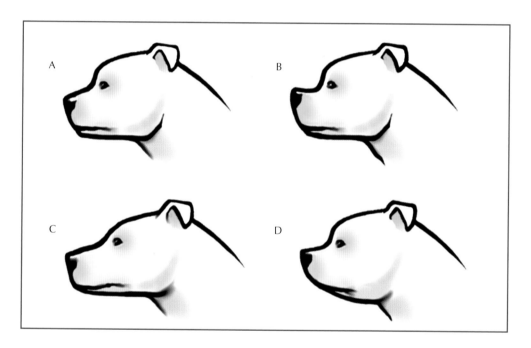

A: Typical (correct) head. B: Dish-faced. C: Shallow. D: Lacking underjaw.

Eyes

Obviously dark is preferred and the part about 'bearing some relation to coat colour' is all right in a fawn or red but amber or 'light' eyes in a black brindle dog can often detract. (Light eyes in particular can give a harsh, 'staring' expression.) On the other hand, how can a white Stafford have eyes that bore any resemablace to his coat colour? What would he have - white eyes?! On this point, whites or pieds have, in the main, the darkest of eyes.

Ears

Again, very important. Of the two types in the Standard, I prefer the rose. Neat, tidy ears with a good ear carriage make a lot of difference to the dog's expression. A dog with large, thick ears is less desirable, especially in a dog bred for fighting, as the ears would make bigger targets for an adversary.

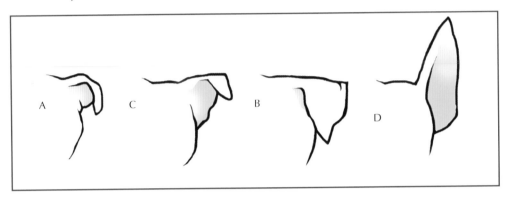

A: Correct ear. B: Half-pricked. C: Drop ear. D: Pricked.

Mouth

Again, in a fighting dog the lips should be 'tight and clean'. If they are not then, once again, a 'lippy' dog offers an opponent a larger target. The teeth also are all-important.

There is nothing more disheartening, especially when judging, than to see a dog or bitch which really takes your eye, only to find when the mouth is examined an undershot mouth or one with badly inverted canines.

Different people place different levels of importance on the bite. In fact, some people rather light-heartedly say, "If a Stafford was hanging from your backside you wouldn't know if it had a bad mouth!" In my opinion, the correct bite is very important in this breed.

Neck

This part of the Standard has in it the word 'rather'. This one word is perhaps one of the reasons

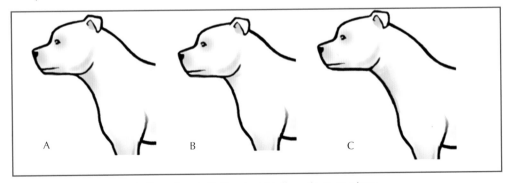

A: Correct neck. B: Too short (stuffy neck). C: Too long.

why the Staffordshire Bull Terrier Standard is so widely interpreted by different judges. For example, one person's interpretation of 'rather short' could well be 'rather' shorter or 'rather' longer than that of another person. Again, in my opinion, a short, muscular neck is vital. After all, the neck is the buffer. It takes the impact.

Forequarters

Also uses the word 'rather'. *Legs straight and well boned, set **rather** wide apart.* Again, judges' interpretations of 'rather wide apart' can be very different. Some 'rather wide apart' legs are too wide and some too narrow. In each case, whatever it may be, that particular person obviously deems his interpretation to be correct.

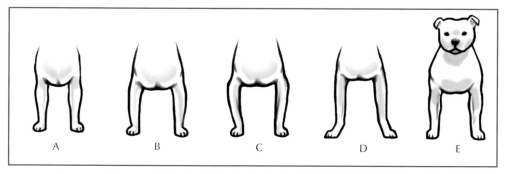

A: Narrow front. B: Wide in front. C: Out at elbow. D: Weak pasterns. E: Correct front.

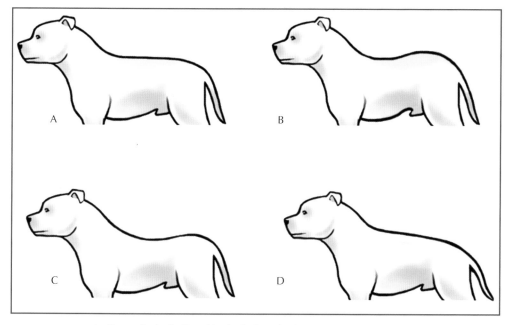

A: Correct body. B: Camel back. C: Sway back. D: Dropping away at rear.

Body

Short back or close coupled, these two things meaning the same. This is the distance between the end of the ribcage and the start of the thighs. Invariably, a short backed dog possesses a strong back. A level topline usually indicates a correct spinal formation. Deep brisket: the brisket or chest should finish at around the same level as the elbows. In general, giving a look of tremendous strength and fitness from any angle.

Hindquarters and Stifles

Again, quite straightforward. Just remember: thighs like hams. The back end should be very muscular and powerful. After all, in the fighting days as now, this is the dog's launch pad!

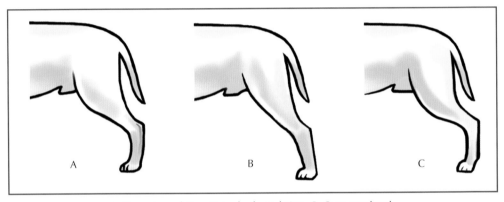

A: Correct angulation. B: Lack of angulation. C: Over-angulated.

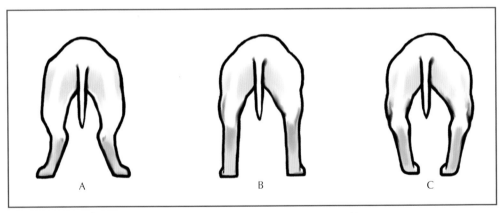

A: Cow hocked. B: Correct hindquarters. C: Barrel leg.

Feet

Again, straightforward.

Tail

Possibly the least important part of the Standard. Although this part is again very straightforward, the allocation of only 5 points in the original Standard's scale of points indicates the importance of the tail from a practical point of view.

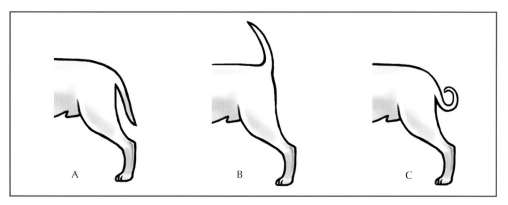

A: Correct tail. B: Gay tail. C: Hook tail.

Gait/Movement

Another controversial subject. Again, how is a Stafford's movement to be assessed? With a dog originally bred for fighting, does its movement actually mean anything at all? In my opinion, a Stafford should have a jaunty gait, move squarely from front and rear and mostly with drive. It is often stated that a dog which is put together right (construction) will move right. Very often, dogs can be seen with varying degrees of sideways movement on their back ends. This sideways or crabbing movement is often referred to as the 'knitting needle syndrome'. Work that one out for yourselves!

Coat

Straightforward. The only thing I would say is that a Stafford that is kept outside will develop a thicker, harsher coat, for obvious reasons. Therefore, if your Stafford is to be shown, it is advisable that he or she is kept indoors.

Correct smooth coat.

Colour

Again, within the restraints of the Standard, any colour is acceptable. No good dog is a bad colour, except liver or black and tan, of course.

Breeders and judges alike are very often pigeon-holed when it comes to colour. By this, I mean that if you have amassed any form of success with a particular colour of Stafford, be it black brindle, red or pied, you will be associated with that particular colour, especially when judging. It is not unusual to see, if the person judging has a preference for a certain colour, that there will be quite a large number of this type of colour exhibits entered under him/her. Of course, the colour should be irrelevant. On this point, I feel white markings enhance a dog's appearance. Pieds in particular are very eye-catching. Very often they stand out in a line-up of solid coloured dogs. Having said this, the specimen is all-important.

Size

This is the most controversial point in this Standard. It will be argued over forever. It is in black and white. Different people put their own slant on it. Rightly or wrongly, that is the case. All I would say on this is that dogs should be masculine and bitches feminine.

Faults

Again, different people apply different levels of importance to different faults. If you try to stick to the Standard and all it entails you should end up with a Stafford that looks pretty decent.

A black and white dog.

A skewbald bitch.

CHAPTER 8

SHOWING

Steve showing Arnie from the side; the black Stafford is being given the lead.

This subject for me is the absolute pinnacle with regards to pedigree dogs. Not just for Staffords but, I imagine, for all breeds of dog.

I will endeavour to start at the very beginning, aiming at the complete novice.

Firstly, I think it is vital that, before you actually enter any show, you do as we did – that

Arnie and his daughter Rockstaff Gipsy Queen.
Left: Judge Mr A Mitchell. Right: Judge Mr J Miller.

is, try to go to as many shows as possible. Alternatively, seek the advice of experienced show people. This will give you a basic idea of what is required.

Taking for granted that you have read and digested the Standard, you should have a basic idea of what an ideal Stafford should look like. Having said that, there is no substitute for actually seeing show dogs in the flesh.

My first experience of any dog show was Crufts 1979 at Earls Court in London. Of course, there are many smaller shows which you may find yourself attending, from Limit up to Championship shows. I can

Leisure Centres are popular venues!

remember a distinct feeling of bewilderment, not just at the number of Staffords gathered in one place but also at the number of stalls and other attractions and, not least, the vast size of the actual venue. Completely overwhelming! And I was only a spectator.

A stand selling dog accessories at an outdoor show.

As I say, your first experience may not be Crufts but, wherever it is, you will get some idea of what a dog show is all about. There are shows practically every week throughout the year, all over the country. Wherever you live, there is bound to be a dog show in your area. They vary from Championship Shows through to Open, Limit, and Exemption Shows.

Before you embark on a show career it would be wise to have a Stafford breeder,exhibitor or, preferably, judge assess your dog to see if it is of show quality. Championship show entry fees are not cheap. Add to that the possible cost of a day off work, fuel, refreshments, a catalogue etc and you will see that it can be an expensive and time consuming hobby.

The smallest and most informal shows are Exemption shows, which are held in aid of a charity or cause with entries being taken on the day. They are usually quite well supported and you will also find novelty classes (most handsome dog, best six legs, dog most like its owner etc) and possibly obedience classes at such shows. They may be advertised in your local press, pet shop, dog club or in the dog papers. They are a good day out for the family because there are often other stalls or attractions, all hoping to relieve you of a little money! Dogs need not be Kennel Club registered to compete at these shows but they have to be pedigree dogs to enter the Pedigree classes.

Taking for granted again that both you and your dog have attended sufficient training classes, the best shows to learn at are probably the Open Shows. Here you will find that the classes are very few and also that the number of dogs entered is quite low. These shows provide a vital training ground, not only for the novice exhibitor but also for the up-and-coming judge. The training or ringcraft classes will definitely hold you in good stead for these occasions but, as you will find, there is nothing like the real thing – competition!

Breed Club Limit Shows are exactly what they say: they are limited to the members of that particular club. To become a member of any breed club, all you need to do is to contact your nearest Staffordshire Bull Terrier Breed Club Secretary, whereupon he or she will be more than willing to help you become a member. A list of current Breed Club Secretaries can be found in Useful Addresses.

Breed Club Open Shows are open to all exhibitors of registered Staffords. Before I go any further I must stress that only Kennel Club registered dogs are allowed to enter any of these shows.

Then comes the most important of all: the Championship Show. This is where The Kennel Club Challenge Certificates (CCs) are on offer. These are often referred to as 'tickets' by show people. Attain three of these under three different judges, with at least one being awarded when your dog is aged 12 months or older, and your dog will be granted the title of Champion (Ch). Sounds easy, doesn't it? Let me assure you that it certainly is not! Especially in Staffords, due to the high number of entries.

Usually at Breed Club Championship Shows there are about 20 classes, 10 for each sex. They are:

Minor Puppy For dogs of 6 and not exceeding 9 calendar months of age on the first day of the show.

Puppy For dogs of 9 and not exceeding 12 calendar months of age on the first day of the show.

Junior For dogs of 6 and not exceeding 18 calendar months of age on the first day of the show.

Maiden For dogs which have not won a Challenge Certificate or a first prize at an Open or Championship Show (Minor Puppy, Special Minor Puppy, Puppy and Special Puppy classes excepted whether restricted or not).

Novice For dogs which have not won a Challenge Certificate or three or more first prizes at Open or Championship Shows (Minor Puppy, Special Minor Puppy, Puppy, Special Puppy classes excepted, whether restricted or not).

Graduate For dogs which have not won a Challenge Certificate or four or more first prizes at Championship Shows in Graduate, Post Graduate, Minor Limit, Mid Limit, Limit and Open classes, whether restricted or not.

Post Graduate For dogs which have not won a Challenge Certificate or five or more first prizes at Championship Shows in Post Graduate, Minor Limit, Mid Limit, Limit and Open classes, whether restricted or not.

Limit For dogs which have not won three Challenge Certificates under three different judges or seven or first prizes in all at Championship Shows in Limit and Open classes confined to the breed whether restricted or not, at shows where Challenge Certificates were offered for the breed.

Open For all dogs of the breed for which the class is provided and eligible for entry at the show.

Veteran For dogs of not less than 7 years of age on the day of the show.

The terminology used in these definitions will become clearer as you read on.

The first thing your dog has to do is to win his or her class. This, in itself, is quite an achievement. Sometimes there can be up to 30 exhibits in one class – perhaps more. Five exhibits are normally placed. This is commonly known as being 'in the cards'.

* First . . . . .Red card or rosette
* Second . . . . .Blue card or rosette

Arnie set up and ready for the judge to go over.

- Third . . . . .Yellow card or rosette
- Fourth or Reserve . . . . .Green card or rosette
- Fifth or VHC (Very Highly Commended) . . . . .White card or rosette

When all the classes have been judged, each of the class winners will assemble once again. This is the 'challenge'. From these unbeaten entries, the judge will choose his Best Dog (Best Bitch in the Bitch classes) who is the Challenge Certificate winner. A Reserve Challenge Certificate winner for each sex will also be chosen.

Usually at these shows the entry is so high that two judges are required: one for dogs and one for bitches.

When both judges have selected their respective CC winners, the winners then come up against each other to ascertain which exhibit will become Best Of Breed (BOB), or Best In Show (BIS). In this instance, the dog judge goes over the winning bitch, and vice versa. If the two judges cannot agree then a referee is brought in and his or her decision is final.

If your exhibit is ever given a BOB or BIS, cherish it dearly. It is a fantastic achievement. When our dog achieved BOB at Crufts in 1995, I think around 320 Staffords were entered. To finish 'top of the tree' is quite an outstanding feeling.

So when I said, "Sounds easy, doesn't it?" now you know why it most certainly is not.

Numerically, Staffords are in the Top Ten in The Kennel Club table of registered dogs (9,563 were registered in 1999 and 332 dogs were shown at Crufts 2000).

Example of an entry form for a Championship show.

If you do not know anyone connected in any way with dog shows then the easiest way to find out about when and where they are being held is to buy a copy of one of the weekly dog papers, *Dog World* or *Our Dogs*. All the forthcoming shows are listed in these. Once you have decided which shows you would like to enter you will need to obtain a schedule for that particular show. The telephone number or address of the Show Secretary is supplied with the advertisement for the show.

Once you have received this you will find all the relevant information about the show: the time it opens, the time judging starts, lists of particular breeds and how many classes are available to those breeds. At Open Shows most classes are for dogs and bitches (mixed classes) unless otherwise stated. The price of entering your dog will also be listed. All societies have show catalogues, which can be paid for in advance with your entry fee. They are slightly cheaper this way. The closing date for entries is also marked clearly on the schedule, usually on the front cover. Very often the directions to the venue are also supplied in the schedule.

Once you have received your schedule just read through it carefully, paying particular attention to the actual entry form. If you have never entered a dog show before, it can be quite confusing when it comes to deciding which class to enter. Refer back to the earlier class definitions for guidance. (In addition, The Kennel Club Year Book defines the classes and contains all The Kennel Club Rules and Regulations with regard to shows and all other dog matters under its jurisdiction. It can be purchased from the Publications Department of The Kennel Club.) If you are still unsure which classes to enter, members of your local ringcraft club should be able to help. You will find by talking to someone experienced in showing that they will be in a better position to give you advice on which class to enter. For instance, as you now know, you cannot show your puppy until it is at least 6 months old.

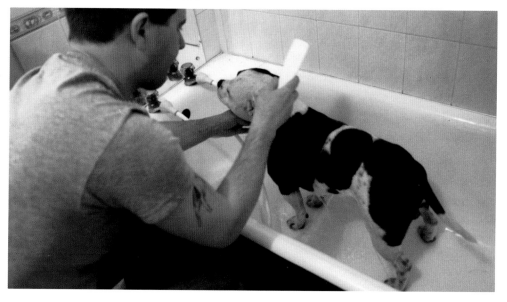

Bathtime for the Breed Record Holder.

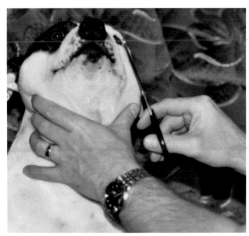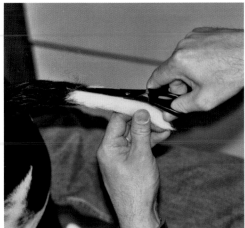

Left: Trimming Arnie's whiskers.
Right: Using scissors to tidy the underside of the tail.

Left: Finishing off the tail with a stripping comb.
Right: A final polish completes the picture.

Having said that, it is no use getting all excited and nervous about showing your 6 month old puppy for the first time if it is nowhere near ready. Some puppies are just not ready for the show ring at 6 months of age. This is where the advice of a more experienced person is invaluable. You will only end up being very disappointed if you start the dog off when he is too immature. Unfortunately, there are quite a number of newcomers whose initial results fail to fall in line with their aspirations and who, unless they are given the correct advice and encouragement at this time, never attend another show. On the other hand, some exhibitors who do not meet with success quickly become even more determined to do so.

Preparing your Stafford for the show ring is relatively easy compared with other breeds. Basically, road work will keep his feet nice and tight, also keeping his nails short. Make sure his ears and teeth are also clean. If you happen to own a pied or predominantly white Stafford then you will find yourself having to bath him far more than you would a dog of a more solid colour. We own pieds and I must admit bathing is a chore which does not rank amongst my favourites. I also trim the dog's whiskers. In my opinion this gives the impression of a cleaner outline. Trimming the underside of the tail also, in my opinion, enhances the appearance of the dog's back end. A nice thin 'whip tail' lends the impression of great strength and muscle tone in the hindquarters. The final thing you can do to enhance the appearance of your dog is to give him a polish with either a leather chamois or a piece of velvet. Special gloves can be purchased for this purpose.

Finally, all this done, the dog in good show condition and trained for the experience, it's off to the show. Just remember one thing: you are asking for one person's opinion of your dog. If this opinion is not to your liking, it is no use getting angry and stamping your feet in a mini-tantrum; the judge will not change his or her mind. You will just be letting yourself and your dog down.

Like your Stafford, you have to have the correct temperament for the show ring. The people who find themselves indulging in this are very quickly labelled bad losers or bad sportsmen. In my opinion, it's just not worth it. Accept your dog's losses with as much grace as his wins and you will be all right. Always remember, the best dog at any show always travels home with you in the back of your car.

Show day

Having bathed your dog and made any necessary grooming preparations beforehand, the big day arrives. Set your alarm early as, unless you are lucky enough to have entered a local show, you may have a fair drive to reach the venue. Also, as a novice on the circuit, you will not be familiar with the venues so should allow yourself extra time to find them. It is always a good idea to allow for things like roadworks, diversions or hold-ups when planning your journey, just in case. If other members of your ringcraft club are also entered at the show, ask if you can follow them, if you are a bit worried about finding the venue by yourself.

Try to have packed everything the night before - including a map, the show schedule, wet weather clothing, your dog's collar, lead, show lead, towel, bowl, water, titbits, brush, grooming glove, folding chair, crate, vet bed, refreshments, bench chain, showground pass, purse, safety pin to hold your ring number and so on. All this can be ready to be loaded into the car on show morning, saving valuable time and avoiding the likelihood of last-minute panics. Filling the car up with petrol beforehand will also save time. Your attire should be smart and complement the dog, so a change of clothes may be necessary before you go in the ring.

Once you arrive at the venue find out where the Stafford rings are located and settle your dog on the bench. (Make sure your dog has had a chance to relieve himself on arrival at the showground - keep those doggy bags handy for picking up.) Keep an eye on the judging and listen to the steward when he announces the next class and the ring numbers of the entrants.

In the ring, stay calm, remember your ringcraft training and make sure your dog enjoys his time in the ring. Talk kindly to him, give him a titbit or word of praise when he has tried to please you and a pat before you leave the ring. (Be discreet if you use food and make sure none is dropped, which could distract other dogs). If it is a large class, you may let your dog relax but make sure you watch the judge so that you know what he expects of you when it is

Left: Positioning the front legs.
Right: Positioning the rear legs.

Checking the view from the front.

your turn. The judge will assess each dog according to the Breed Standard. He does this by examining the dog in the show stance and then seeing the dog on the move. **Staffords are always set up facing the judge** (unlike most breeds which are set up in profile so the judge initially sees them sideways on before moving in for a closer look).

Setting up

There are two ways of setting your Stafford up in the show ring. If you have one that stands still once he has been set up then you can stand at the back of him out of the way so that the judge can see everything. I call this 'giving them the lead'. If on the other hand you have one who fidgets and moves about once set up, you will find yourself crouched down at the side of him, reassuring and giving confidence all the time.

I find that the best way for setting a Stafford up for a show stance is to stand over the top of him with him between your legs. Then lift him up slightly by his brisket (chest). This will allow the front legs to hang freely and also square from the shoulders. Ensure that when the feet are put back down the legs are still square, as they were when suspended.

Ready for the judge.

Left: Moving away from the judge.
Right: Movement in profile.

The final impression.

Once you have sorted the front end then move to the hindquarters. The back end should not be hunched up or over-stretched. The best way to ensure neither of these occur is to make sure that back legs from the feet to the hocks are at right angles to the floor. If the back feet are too far under the dog, a hunched up stance will be given. If they are too far back then an over-stretched impression will be given. The term 'stood four-square' is very relevant to the Stafford: a leg at each corner, so to speak. Once you have him stood four-square there are two alternatives: you can either crouch down at the side of your dog or, as I have previously stated, you give him the lead. Again, this will depend on the dog.

Very often with Arnie I found myself having to do both. It depended on what mood he was in. Either way, you must always try to show your Stafford to his or her full potential and always

A good exhibitor keeps out of the judge's way whilst still maintaining control of their dog.

Observing the dogs from other bloodlines may benefit your own kennel one day.

remember that you – or your Stafford, with a little help from you – are there to impress the judge.

On the move

Once the judge has been over the dog, he will wish to see it moved. This is usually achieved by the handler walking the dog at a trot in a triangle and then a straight line. In this way the judge can assess the dog's movement from different angles. Use the whole ring for the triangle, trotting your dog into the corners. You will learn the correct pace for your dog at ringcraft classes and can even use a mirror or camcorder to assess what you are doing.

Always keep the dog between yourself and the judge (otherwise you will be blocking the judge's view of the dog) and do not allow the dog to pull sideways on the lead, thus spoiling his movement.

At the end of the day

If you can, stay and watch the judging of the other classes. Look at the dogs the judge selects and ask yourself why they were considered superior to the others. Ask questions of your fellow exhibitors, learn as much as you can. (Do not ask them when they are preparing to go in the ring, however. Choose your moment wisely!) Study your catalogue and see where the winning dogs come from. Look at their backgrounds; one day you might need the use of a stud dog from their kennels!

CHAPTER 9

BREEDING

Sooner or later you may find yourself attracted to and having a go at breeding. On this subject I would advise that you consult an experienced breeder for advice on which stud dog to use. Other than that, if you see a dog that really takes your eye, approach the owners and ask about using him.

The best place to see a lot of Staffords is at a Breed Club Championship Show. This is where you will be able to see the best dogs our breed has to offer. If you cannot make it to any show or do not know anyone in the breed, the easiest way to find out about a dog for use at stud is to contact the Secretary of your nearest Staffordshire Bull Terrier Club. A list of current Secretaries is supplied in Useful Addresses.

Explain your intentions to the Secretary. He or she will probably ask you for a few details about your bitch; for example, how is she bred? We have had quite a few stud engagements through this method. Someone will ring up saying, "So and so has put me in touch with you regarding mating my bitch." The arrangements are then taken on from there.

Don't be too eager to have your bitch mated. If you can't use the dog you really want to for some reason, then don't mate her at this stage. Don't use just any stud just for convenience.

If you are a first-time breeder, you may well find yourself being dissuaded from using a certain stud dog and it is usually by the stud dog owner themselves. Certain stud dog owners will only allow certain bitches to be serviced by their dog. They are not being funny, it is just that after a few years of breeding and establishing a line, you can almost guarantee the outcome of a mating, not only for colour but also for type. I say 'almost' because nothing is 100% certain. One thing that is predictable, though, is colour. A black brindle bitch put to a

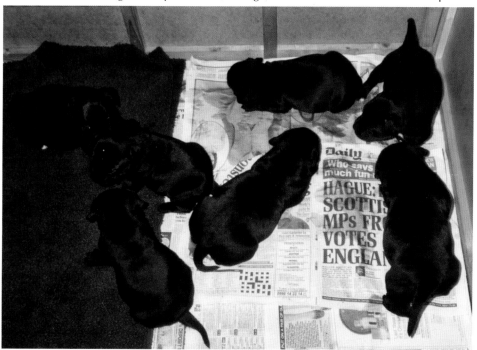

Breeding is a lifetime responsibility.

Ch Black Tusker - the Breed Record Holder for the most Champions sired (sixteen).

black brindle dog will produce black brindle puppies. The same is true of reds. Any of these pups could be solid black or red, or may well have white markings somewhere on them. Pieds usually have equal amounts of white and one other colour. Red and white pieds are referred to as skewbald. Arnie is a black, brindle and white pied and has had every colour under the sun put to him. When using a pied dog, the colour outcome is uncertain. Arnie has thrown every colour possible - not only pieds but also some solid reds and black brindles. So if you have a pied bitch you may find that owners of black brindle or red dogs may not be very keen on letting you use their dogs at stud.

Before selecting a stud it is important to assess your own bitch first. If you have a half decent bitch you should be able to use most dogs. Don't forget that all bitches have their bad points as well as their good ones. Try to find a dog which compliments your bitch, strengthening her qualities and, hopefully, being able to improve on her weak points. However, let me just say that we have had to correct some bitch owners' assumptions that using our stud dog will automatically produce puppies which carry none of their mother's faults. It takes two to tango, after all. We have found that the stud dog will get the blame if the pups are mediocre and the praise if an outstanding pup is produced!

You should also research your bitch's pedigree and that of the prospective stud dog before going ahead with the mating. First-time owners will benefit from the services of an experienced breeder here.

The three main types of breeding are Inbreeding, Line breeding and outcrossing.

• Inbreeding is the closest form of breeding possible; it involves mating two very closely related individuals such as mother-son or father-daughter. This should only be attempted by experienced breeders. Good qualities are fixed by inbreeding but so are bad and they may be difficult to eliminate, so there is no chance of success if two inferior animals are used.

• Line breeding is the mating of related stock such as grandmother to grandson or uncle to niece. A quality line can be produced over time, if only desirable offspring are used from each litter. It is less risky than inbreeding and the resulting dogs will look alike as adults so a particular line will be recognised.

• Outcrossing is the mating of two totally unrelated individuals. Outcrossing is necessary in a breeding programme to introduce new blood or a new characteristic into a line. The progeny should then be mated back to the original line.

Once you have made up your mind on your choice of stud, the next step is to make arrangements with the stud dog owner. The owner may well want to have a look at your bitch first and to be given a copy of your bitch's pedigree and registration document. This is the most important thing: proof that your bitch is registered at The Kennel Club. Some owners of stud dogs may also insist that your bitch has been eye tested.

It is always advantageous and courteous to the stud dog owner to keep him or her informed on what's happening. For instance, when people contact me to ask about a stud I always ask them to let me know the first day they see any sign of blood on their bitch. Then we take it from there.

Mating

The books tell us that bitches are ready for mating any time between the 10th and the 14th day of the season. There are no hard and fast rules on this, as all bitches are different. It is generally the 11th or 13th day, but one of our own bitches was mated on her 21st day and went on to produce three beautiful puppies.

If the right day is selected it makes it easier for all concerned. If the bitch is not quite ready, mating can become quite a fiasco!

In the majority of cases the bitch is taken to the stud dog. This is advantageous to the stud dog, as he will be in familiar surroundings. When all the groundwork has been done, ie a dog, date and time have been selected, it's time for the action to begin.

If your bitch is to be mated for the very first time she is termed a 'maiden bitch' (basically, a virgin). First time bitches, in my opinion, should not be mated until at least their second or third seasons – ideally, third. By this time the bitch will be around 18 months old and not only physically mature but also mentally. We have heard of cases where a bitch was mated on her first season - aged 10 months! This is very bad practice in my opinion and can affect the pups. Please be patient and wait.

If your bitch is a maiden, it would be helpful if the stud dog you have chosen is experienced in this field. If the mating pair do not get on, they will start fighting. You can't just put two Staffords together and expect them to mate. Sometimes we have been able to let Arnie 'free mate' a bitch (no help from me) but this is very rare. Most people in Staffords know what to expect when it comes to mating - there will probably be snarling and growling. Very often a muzzle is the safest option.

A good stud dog is generally good at his job. If the dog you have selected happens to be, like your bitch, a 'virgin', it would be advisable if someone with an in-depth experience of these matters is on hand.

When people come to use our dog we always put him out in the run at least 15 minutes before the arranged arrival time. The people then come in with their bitch. We always give the bitch a little time to familiarise herself with the new surroundings. During this period, vast amounts of tea and coffee are drunk! This not only gives the bitch time to calm down, particularly after a long journey, but also gives the owners of both the bitch and the stud dog time to get to know one another. This is especially useful if you have only spoken to each other on the telephone.

Next the bitch is taken out to empty herself. Believe me, this is a very worthwhile move.

Side view of bitch being held.

The bitch owner keeps a firm grip (both hands) on the collar.

The initial meeting.

We have had visiting bitches whose owners have assured us that their bitch has 'been', only to have her decide to empty herself when the dogs are tied. Not a pleasant sight! If the bitch is a maiden bitch I always wash my hands thoroughly and then apply some lubricant (KY Gel or similar) to my middle finger and gently insert it into her vagina. In my opinion, this is better for the bitch in that it breaks her in steadily rather than letting the dog thrust away at her immediately.

The owner of the bitch is always in charge of the bitch. This is better for the bitch as she will not then have an unfamiliar face glaring at her. The bitch should wear a strong collar that can be gripped. Then the person in charge of the bitch should grip each side of the collar so that the bitch cannot turn her head around and bite the dog.

Some people allow their dogs to roam about together in a sort of 'love play' mode. Although this is supervised, we do not advocate it. No matter how placid your bitch is, if she takes a dislike to the chosen stud dog or vice versa, the next thing you will be doing is trying to separate a pair of fighting Staffords rather than supervising a pair of mating Staffords.

As mentioned above, if a bitch is particularly nasty, we muzzle her, just to be on the safe side. You can use any ordinary muzzle, which can be purchased at any pet shop. Alternatively, you can use a crepe bandage, as I do, or a pair of old tights. To do this, wrap one or the other around the bitch's muzzle a few times with sufficient tightness to prevent her from opening her jaws and then pass it through the collar and secure it in a tight knot. Do not worry: although this is a strange experience for your bitch, her air passages are still clear, so her breathing is not affected in any way at all. As soon as a tie has been achieved and the dogs are back-to-back, the muzzle can be taken off.

The initial mounting. Note the need to support the bitch as she tries to lower down.

Now to the 'tie'. A tie is not always necessary to produce puppies. In fact, some stud dog owners will not let their dogs tie. A tie is just proof that the dog is releasing sperm. Like I said earlier, however, a tie does not always produce puppies.

About three quarters of the way down the dog's penis is what is referred to as the 'knot'. If you imagine something in the region of the size of a golf ball then you are visualising the knot. When the dog is at full arousal his thrusting motion will speed up dramatically. It is at this point that the knot is inserted into the bitch. Once it is in, the bitch grips hold – and the dogs are tied. We always leave the dog on top of the bitch for a few minutes to allow her to tighten up around the knot before we turn the

Left: Checking that the stud dog has penetrated.
Right: Supporting the stud dog.

Left: During the tie, the two heads are in very close proximity, hence the need to restrain the bitch.
Right: Slowly allowing the dog to turn.

dog. Sometimes, when we have attempted to turn the dog too early, the knot has come out mid-turn.

When 3–4 minutes have elapsed, gently slide one of the dog's front legs across the shoulders of the bitch, and then ease his back leg over her as well. They will now be in a back-to-back position. Having achieved this, the main job now is just to concentrate on the bitch to make sure she doesn't make any sudden movements, thus injuring herself or the dog. The length of the tie is determined by the bitch. She will release the dog when she is ready.

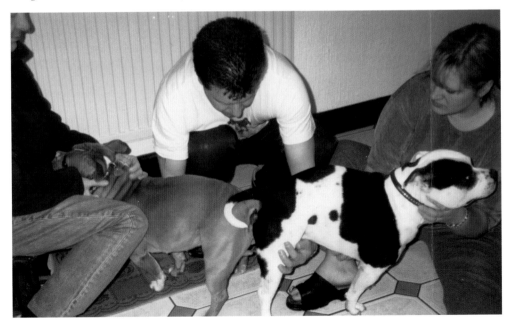

Now the dog is fully turned.

Ties can vary in time but generally last 20–30 minutes. Having said that, we have experienced ties that have lasted from 10 minutes minimum to 2 hour 20 minutes maximum. This was quite an ordeal for us. The first thing that was different on this particular day was that Sam, our trusted helper, was not available, so Julie and I had to get on with it ourselves. The actual mating went like a dream. So there we were, dogs tied, back to back, us talking about doggy things. The 20-minute mark came in with a flash, then half an hour, then 45 minutes. At this point I wasn't worried as the bitch previous to this one had been tied for an hour. Anyway, the hour mark came and went. By the time an hour and a half had passed I was beginning to get worried. With no Sam on hand for advice, I decided to telephone our vet. He just said, "Don't panic – let Nature take its course. They'll come apart when they're ready." Having heard this we were all somewhat relieved. Watching the dogs carefully I noticed that our dog was actually falling asleep on his feet, still tied! We all found this very amusing. At this point, I gently laid both dogs down on their side, whereupon they promptly went to sleep.

Sure enough, just like our vet had said, nature took its course and, after almost two and a half hours, the bitch released the dog, much to my relief. Nine weeks later the bitch produced five healthy puppies.

As I said earlier, there are no hard and fast rules when it comes to dogs.

Gestation

Once your bitch has been mated the gestation period is usually 63 days. This is not always the case though, especially with maiden bitches. Having said that, it is not always maiden bitches who 'come down' early.

Supporting the dog and bitch during the tie.

The average tie may last 25-30 minutes.

One of our bitches, Ginnie (Arnie's mother), 6 years of age at the time and also an experienced mother, having had three previous litters, really caught us unawares! She was due to whelp on the Friday, which was her 63rd day, so every thing was being geared up for that date. On the Sunday evening, her 58th day, we noticed that she was very restless and panting profusely. Ginnie always showed similar symptoms when a storm was approaching, which was the case that night. After quite a while, Julie said, "I think she'll whelp tonight."

Impossible, I thought. *She's 5 days early.*

Impossible? No, quite wrong!

My father-in-law had borrowed our whelping box a few months earlier so I had decided to go and fetch it on the Monday, which was still 4 days early. Circumstances on this particular Sunday proved otherwise – I had to fetch it immediately! Whilst we were preparing the area, a loud yelp came from one of the other rooms. The room in question was in fact the room where I had put Ginnie while the whelping area was made ready. We both rushed in to see what was happening. To our horror, there was Ginnie licking away at the membrane in which her first puppy had arrived.

This little personal experience just goes to prove that even bitches who have had litters previously can whelp' early. Luckily, the puppy was all right and his four brothers and one sister were whelped in the more orthodox manner. You have to be prepared and have everything ready at a week to 10 days before the due date. This is just to be on the safe side and hopefully avoid a mishap akin to the one I have just described.

Before things get to the latter stages of the pregnancy, the 9 week gestation period should give you adequate time to get a number of things ready, especially if you have never had a litter before.

The first thing you must decide is where your bitch is going to have her litter. This is of vital importance, also as much for your sake as for the bitch. I say this because for the first 72 hours at least you must be prepared to say with the new puppies in a sort of puppy-watch mode. It is at this stage that the puppies are at their most vulnerable. Staffords are generally good mothers but you never know. It is always better to be safe than sorry.

Normal exercise can be taken by the expectant mother up to 5–6 weeks into the pregnancy. After this time just be careful, making sure that she doesn't take any unnecessary knocks or bangs which could cause damage to the unborn puppies. In fact, the exercise could be almost completely cut out at this stage.

We always whelp our bitches in one of the spare bedrooms. This enables either Julie or myself to sleep at the side of the puppies so that any unforeseen problems can be attended to in seconds. It is a very tiring and trying time but, if together with your bitch you can manage to rear all your puppies, the feeling of achievement is fantastic.

The main benefit of whelping in the house is that the place will already be warm. This again is not only for the puppies but also for you. Believe me, it's no fun trying to get to sleep in a shed or outbuilding in mid-November!

If a shed or outbuilding is the only place you have available for whelping than a heat bulb or infra-red lamp is a 'must'. This is placed 18–24in from the base of the whelping box. It is left on all the times and ensures that the puppies are always warm.

4–5 weeks after the mating it should become apparent if your bitch is in whelp. Her teats will have become larger as well as her loin area showing added girth.

You will also find that by this time your bitch will have become greedier, eating considerably more than normal. Obviously she is eating for more than herself.

About a fortnight before the due date, introduce her to where she is going to have the puppies. In particular, get her used to the whelping box. Entice her into the box. You'll probably find she'll jump in anything just to be nosy! Maybe get her to sit or lie down in it. After a while she might even go to sleep in it. This is all a good familiarisation period. Don't forget that the whelping box is your bitch's new living quarters for at least 6 weeks after whelping.

Also in the interim period, you will need to collect as many old newspapers as you can. These are for the actual time of whelping. This, as will become abundantly clear, is quite a messy time. After every birth, the soiled newspapers must be discarded and replaced with clean papers. It is also

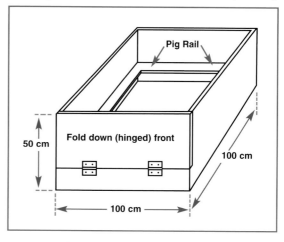

Plan of a home-made whelping box.

advisable to inform your vet well in advance of the impending litter. Inform him or her about a fortnight before the due date, just as a matter of courtesy. It is wise to avoid understandable annoyance if his or her services have to be called upon, especially in the early hours, if you hit problems. Although, as I said earlier, Staffords are generally good mothers and whelpers, so hopefully you'll be all right.

Whelping

You will know when your bitch is about to whelp. In the last day or so, her temperature should drop (from 101.5°F to around 98-99°F, or from 38.6°C to 36.7-37.2°C) and she may well be off her food. Some bitches are more clingy as well. Your bitch's obvious restlessness, panting and relentless scratching at the newspapers in the bottom of the whelping box will also warn you of the imminent births. At this stage, you should be sat at the side of the whelping box supervising everything. This is also a good time to ring your vet and let him know what is happening in case you have need of him (it is also polite to ring when whelping has finished, just to let him know that all has gone okay and he will not be required). This is a private time for the bitch, so do not let anyone else in the whelping area other than is strictly needed.

You will see your bitch straining, perhaps three or four times, before a puppy is produced. It is vitally important that you keep your eye on the bitch from the very first purge or straining movement. If the bitch has pushed a few times and nothing seems to be happening I wash my hands thoroughly and then insert my index finger gently into the bitch's vulva. You should at

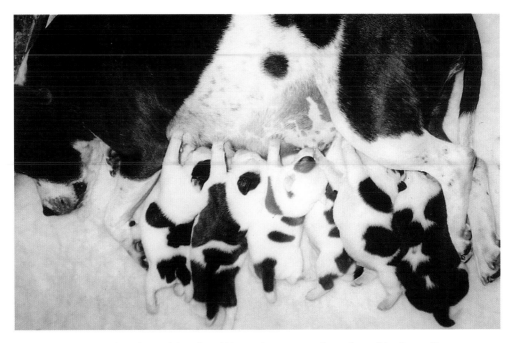

Contented mother with her day old litter. The pups are clean, dry and feeding well.

some point be able to feel the puppy's head. If you can, remember the distance your finger has been inserted. Having witnessed maybe one or two more pushes and still no puppy, repeat the procedure. With each push the puppy should be travelling nearer and nearer to the end of the birth canal. Obviously, if your finger can be inserted the same distance after several pushes then the puppy is not moving along as it should be. In these circumstances, always call your vet immediately.

When the first puppy arrives, it will be in its membranous sac. At this point the bitch will tear open the sac and also sever the umbilical cord, which attaches the puppy to its placenta (afterbirth). Having said that, I always tear open the sac myself and also cut the umbilical cord. I do this with a sharp pair of sterilised scissors, the cut being made at least 2in from the pup's stomach. The umbilical cord will eventually dry up and drop off. If the bitch is allowed to sever the cord, she could get carried away and go too close to the puppy's stomach resulting in a ruptured naval.

The bitch will then 'get the pup going' by licking it and knocking it about a bit until it is completely clean. This again can be done by you and is something I always do. A firm rubbing and drying off with a piece of towelling acts as a more-than-equal substitute for the mother's tongue. Each puppy should be followed by its placenta. If it isn't, don't be too alarmed. You will see the cord hanging from the vulva. A gentle pull will bring it out of the bitch. The bitch will also want to eat the afterbirth. This is fine, but it is up to you whether you permit her to eat all of them (they can cause diarrhoea if eaten to excess). When the puppy is in a clean state put it on to a teat and allow it to suckle.

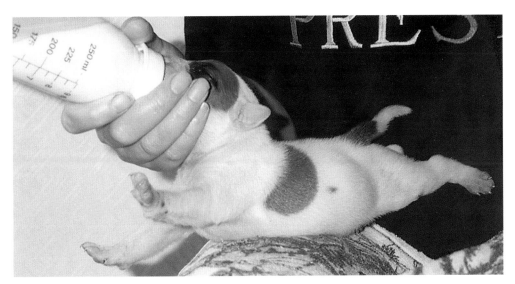

Large litters can be supplemented with bottle feeding.

When another birth is imminent, remove the first born puppy and place it on the covered hot water bottle, preferably in a cardboard box. This ensures that the first puppy will not get messed up again. When the second pup has been dealt with in the same way, place them both back on to the teats. Repeat this for every birth. Don't forget that after every birth there will be quite a lot of mess so constant changing of the newspapers is vital.

Once your bitch settles off she will perhaps go to sleep. This is a good sign that she has finished whelping. You may find that when all the pups have been born your bitch is continually picking them up and moving them, sometimes completely out of the whelping box! This is usually down to nervousness. Gently but firmly dissuade her from doing so. If not, consult your vet. Make sure that all the pups are placed on the teats so that they all get their fair share of the milk. Obviously, they are not always feeding and very often the teats are just used as dummies.

Always keep your eye out for the 'rickling' (the weakest member of the litter) for he or she will be easily knocked off the teats and consequently miss out on the milk.

If your bitch has six or more pups it is always helpful if you can supplement her when it comes to feeding the litter. Again, we always do this. Goat's milk, we have found, is absolutely fantastic for this purpose. There are other milk substitutes that can be used but we find goat's milk to be superior. We buy it from the local farm. It is purchased in pints and can be either fresh or frozen. We buy both: the fresh obviously to be used immediately and the frozen to be put straight into the freezer, a pint being thawed out every night for usage the following day.

The puppies are fed in just the same way as feeding a baby. A feeding bottle and teat can be purchased from any chemist. Fill the bottle with goat's milk, then place it in a jug of boiling water and let it heat up in this way. Test its temperature by sprinkling some on to the back of your hand or forearm. Never feed them with it when it is too hot. When it's just warm, proceed to feed (see photo above)

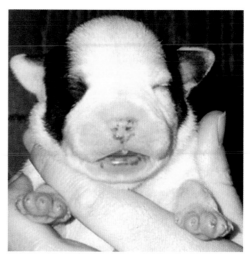

Four day old puppies. Note the lack of pigment in their noses at this age.

This again is probably not done by all breeders but we do it and find it is a tremendous help in giving extra nourishment to the puppies as well as supplementing your bitch so that she is not dragged down too much. Feeding like this is done every 2–3 hours and always in conjunction with normal feeding from the mother.

The day after the puppies have been born I also strongly advise you to have what I call a 'clear-out injection' given to your bitch. This injection will get rid of any retained placentas. If they are left inside the bitch they could poison her and also her milk, thus killing the puppies. As you can see, this is a vital injection. It is also wise to ask the vet to give your bitch the once-over after she has whelped. This may be best performed at home so that you do not risk the bitch coming into contact with unwell animals at the surgery

All puppies are born blind. They are also born with completely pink noses. After 4–5 days you will notice the pink noses becoming speckled with black spots (pigment). This is quite normal and by the time the pups are 3–4 weeks old their noses should be completely black.

When the puppies are anything from 10–13 days old you should be witnessing the eyes opening. By the times 18–19 days have passed the first teeth should be breaking through.

Weaning

We also wean the pups as soon as possible. This is not strictly essential but it does help the bitch. When the puppies are first introduced to non-milk foods they should be about 3 weeks old. If you have never seen pups lapping for the first time, let me assure you that it is very amusing. Obviously, they have never seen or tasted custard or rice pudding before. Whatever it is you decide to try them on first, simply warm it up and put it on to a plate or shallow dish. Then put it into the whelping box and observe! The first thing the pups will do probably is to stampede straight through it! By the time the first session is over, the pups will probably be totally covered in food. Just give them a wipe down with a damp cloth. It does get better from here on!

Being weaned on to cooked minced beef.

Enjoying a meal of scrambled egg.

The best way to introduce them to lapping is to smear some of the food around their mouths. This way they'll be able to taste and smell it more easily. Hopefully, then they'll follow the aroma straight to the dish. The meals could be as follows: two milk feeds, two meat feeds – at least four meals a day as well as mother's milk. For instance:

8am

A dish of custard, rice pudding, porridge, Ready Brek or similar (any of which to be warmed).

12 noon

A meat meal consisting of minced beef and gravy or tinned puppy food with some small-bite mixer.

4pm

Repeat the 8.00 am meal.

8pm

Repeat the 12.00 noon meal.

Before you settle them down for the night, a dish of warm milk can be given. This should help them to sleep through the night.

As you will have gathered, rearing puppies is not cheap but the more goodness you put into them at this age the more you stand them in good stead for an active and healthy adulthood.

Practically all puppies develop worms and the youngsters will not thrive properly until this parasite is eliminated. Faeces that are jelly-like are the usual symptoms. Worming treatment can be obtained from your vet or any pet shop. At this age you will require roundworm tablets only. Tapeworm treatment is not required until the pups have reached 6 months of age.

We always worm puppies (roundworm) at 4, 6, 8, 10 and 12 weeks. Do tell the new owners about the worming timetable and what has already been administered. Instructions will be on the box of tablets. The amount given is always dependent on the weight of the puppy. The easiest way to give them is to place each tablet or part-tablet at the back of the pup's

Five weeks old - weaned, wormed and ready for mischief.

throat, close the muzzle and hold it shut while gently rubbing the throat. The rubbing action will ensure that the puppy will swallow the tablet.

The worms usually come out in a tight, writhing ball. Very often there are more worms than faeces. I have only witnessed bad roundworms once and I put this down to not starting the worming program until the pups were about 7 weeks old. One of the pups was playing around at the back of the sofa when he started sniffing and spinning around, so there was I with kitchen roll in hand ready for the impending mess. When it came, I nearly died! I thought "He's been eating the tassels on the edge of the carpet." On closer inspection, they were not stringy tassels but wriggling roundworms! Yuk! So, be warned: if you are a little squeamish you won't be eating spaghetti for quite some time once you have witnessed a puppy with roundworms.

Growing pups find plenty to do and will appreciate the most basic of toys.

Explorers!

Socialisation

Socialising your puppies is very important. Whether your pups go to show or pet homes, it is important that they are equipped to deal with the outside world. From the age of 5 or 6 weeks our pups are allowed to go anywhere they want, within reason. It is quite amusing to see a litter of pups running around on the lawn with the other adults Staffords. The adults seem to revert back to puppyhood themselves when surrounded by the youngsters. It is also important that the pups get used to being handled by other people (of both sexes). Ours come into the house to find out about different noises, such as the washing machine, hoover, television, telephone and so on. All this helps to prepare them for their new homes.

When it comes to interviewing prospective owners, Julie has a sixth sense for sussing people out. If she is not happy with someone, they do not leave with one of our pups. Litters can be advertised in the dog press or the local paper. Word of mouth may be sufficient to sell your litter; we are lucky in this respect because people are ringing us all the time for pups. Again, this is solely down to Arnie's success. Once you have a reputation as a good breeder, selling your pups is no problem. We let people look at the pups when they are 3-4 weeks old. They pick the one they want and then we ask for a deposit. This is important as a deposit secures. In the past we have had people say "Keep that one for me" only to find that, when it's time for the puppy to be collected, they have changed

Nearly ready to leave the nest.

95

their mind. Once a deposit has been left, the balance is paid on collection. This is normally around 8 weeks of age. They will also receive a diet sheet (including timetable), a pedigree and the Kennel Club Registration form, if we have received this back from The Kennel Club. Finally, the new owners are assured of our assistance at any time.

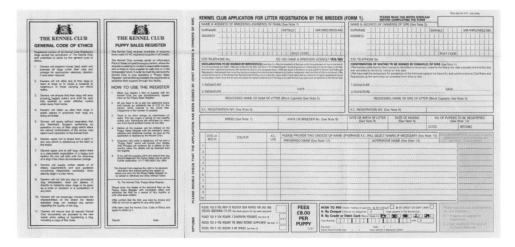

The Kennel Club Litter Registration Form (F1).
The breeder is the only person who is allowed to register the litter.

Handrearing a Litter

Before I start on this subject, let me just say that if you had asked me six months previous to this experience, I would have said that there are no bad Stafford mothers. I have already touched upon it by saying that Staffords are generally good mothers. Again, let me stress that they are. Of course there are always exceptions to the rule as we now know from experience.

Years ago, my father-in-law had Bull Terriers. He didn't know it at the time, but they aren't very good with their offspring. Anyway, to cut a long story short, he decided to breed from one of his bitches. The bitch was mated and consequently whelped a litter. Everything seemed fine. When the pups were around 4 weeks old, something very shocking happened. (Bear in mind that when pups reach this age the time for worrying is usually over.)

Eric had been out, leaving mother and pups in the confines of their kennel. When he returned he went down to check on the litter. To his surprise, there were only 2 pups, not 4. He searched everywhere for them, to no avail. They were nowhere to be seen. His first thought was that they had been stolen. A closer look at the mother revealed everything. On her lips were signs of something red. When Eric opened her mouth he found traces of blood and fur. The dam had actually killed and eaten two of her offspring! Eric took her straight away to the vet, almost expecting to have her put down. However, the vet informed him that this occurrence was quite commonplace in the breed and there was no need to have the bitch destroyed. Once Bull Terriers have whelped, the pups should be removed from their mother and only taken back to feed off her under supervision. Unfortunately my father-in-law found out the hard way.

I'm not saying all Bull Terriers are like this but a couple who live nearby breed and show them and every litter they have basically has to be handreared. Their advice was invaluable to us when we encountered this problem. Until very recently I would have put money on a Stafford being an excellent mother. Now we know that the opposite can occur I will tell you about our own experience with a bitch who rejected her litter.

To put you in the picture, Sammy was a very nice all white Stafford bitch. She was bred and owned by us but lived with my parents. When Sammy was two we all agreed, because she was a decent specimen, to breed from her. We were hoping for a nice bitch puppy to continue the line. So, after some debate, a stud dog was selected, one that tied in with our line. Sammy was taken to be mated twice, on her 12th and 14th day. Both trips were very successful with twenty minute ties. After six weeks it was obvious that Sammy was definitely in whelp and preparations were made for the forthcoming litter. The only thing that was different for us was that the litter would be born and reared at my parents house, not ours.

On the day of the whelping everything was fine. Sammy had six beautiful red and red/white pups - 3 dogs and 3 bitches. She gave birth to all of them with ease. In fact all six were born within four hours. Just after midnight, she began to fall asleep, with the pups still suckling from her. Job done, we thought. My parents had enjoyed whelping their bitch (with help from us, of course!). The only thing left to do now was to take Sammy to the vet for a check over and a clear out jab. So the next day my father took her to the vet who checked that her womb had contracted and everything was okay. The problems started when he arrived back home. My parents had to go out so Julie was left in charge of the pups. This is usually a very easy job. Its just a case of being there at the side of the whelping box in case the mother decides to lie on and consequently squash any of the pups. Julie has done this many times before, as we both have, without encountering any problems. As Julie was sitting in the chair beside the whelping box, she noticed that Sammy had started to growl. This started off quite quietly, with an occasional rumble and graduated to loud frequent rumbling. In most cases a stern talking to usually does the trick and things settle down again. (Sometimes a first-time mother can be a little bemused when dealing with the puppies but after a day or so she gets used to the idea of what her responsibilities are and gets on with it). It seemed that every time the pups were crawling about, particularly underneath Sammy, this made the growling worse. Having never seen this before on such a scale, Julie became quite worried. She did not know what Sammy was going to do.

When my parents arrived home they, too, were alarmed by the normally placid Sammy's behaviour. Another stern talking to by my father proved to have no effect at all. I arrived a few hours later after work and could not believe what I was seeing: a Stafford rejecting her puppies. When you have never been in a situation like this before, it is very difficult to work out what is happening and, more importantly, what to do. The first I thing I though of was to phone some very good friends who had been in the breed for over 30 years to seek their advice. They said that some bitches can react like this but after a couple of days or so they should be okay. We had also thought this but it wasn't the case. I then phoned the stud dog owners, another couple

This litter was handreared by Steve and Julie Bradder from the age of 6 days.

who had also been in Staffords for over 30 years. They told us that they had had a bitch like this some years ago. Eventually her pups had to be taken away and handreared. With every passing hour we were beginning to realise that this was what we were going to have to do. This still did not answer the question, "Why?" As a last resort I phoned our vet and explained what had happened. He told me how Bull Terriers react, which we were already aware of, but which we had not seen before in Staffords.

I went down to his surgery at 10.30pm that night. The puppies were now 3 days old. The vet prescribed some tranquillisers and liquid to guard against calcium deficiency, to go on Sammy's food. The first sign of calcium deficiency in Bull Terriers is aggression by the dam either towards her litter or people. We dosed Sammy up but the tranquillisers just knocked her out whilst the liquid calcium had no effect at all. The next morning my father and Julie took Sammy to the vet's. He could not find anything wrong with her and could only suggest that we take the puppies away from the mother for safety reasons. We had tried to think of any reason which would explain Sammy's behaviour. We even wondered if Sammy was jealous of the puppies, because she was such a one-man dog (she was never away from my father's side). Perhaps she felt threatened by the puppies? At times it was hard to know whether she was growling at us or them. Either way, it was very, very frightening.

On the morning of the pups being 6 days old, my father rang at 6am. He was practically speechless, at his wits end. He was almost in tears on the other end of the phone. The thing to bear in mind was that for six days and nights my parents had had no sleep and were stressed out of their minds. My father had to sit beside the whelping box holding Sammy by the collar in case she attacked one of the puppies, because no one knew what she would do. Things were now so desperate that we decided to take the pups up to our house, away from Sammy. It was not fair on my parents, no one should have to go through that. Now the handrearing had to begin. As I have mentioned earlier, we always supplement the feeding, especially with large litters. So bottle feeding goats milk was nothing new for us. What was new was completely assuming the mother's role. This was very weird to begin with. Six puppies, six days old, all in the whelping box in the spare bedroom but no mother. The biggest worry was making the pups empty after feeding. This is where our Bull Terrier friends' help was invaluable, because they were so experienced. Making the pups wee is relatively easy. In fact, just the action of crawling about on their stomachs in the whelping box will stimulate them to urinate. Making them defecate is a different matter though. The action of the mother's tongue must be mimicked. After each puppy has been fed it is vitally important that each one is made to defecate. This is done by soaking little cotton wool balls in olive oil, squeezing out the excess oil and then rubbing the puppy's backside with it. This stimulates the bowels, resulting in the pup producing a motion. Doing the same thing to the belly makes the pup urinate.

The pups had to be individually fed and emptied every two to three hours. We used a small box beside the whelping box to place each puppy in once it had been attended to. Once the whole litter had been done, they were returned to the whelping box to sleep. As the puppies grew, they needed more milk. I was usually on the night shift so if I started feeding at midnight, by the time each one had been fed and emptied it was nearly 2am. Time for the first one to be fed again! Sleep was at a premium! After feeding each one, the puppy was held in my left hand whilst I stimulated its bladder and bowel with the cotton wool in my right hand. By the time you have done this six times every two to three hours, you think your arms are going to drop off. In normal circumstances the weaning process starts at around three weeks old and, believe me, when you have handreared a litter, you cannot wait for this time. Eventually, after a couple of weeks, the puppies gradually to start to go to the toilet by themselves after feeding. This is fantastic because no more arm aching stimulation needs to be given. It is advisable thought to make sure that each pup is vacating its bowels. Handrearing is very tiring and challenging and I sincerely hope we never have to do it again. Before I forget, Sammy was her normal self after the pups were taken away from her. One word of warning: don't forget that the mother is making milk and will continue to produce it. It is of great importance that this milk is drained off her or she may get mastitis. The undrained milk congeals and makes one or more of the teats very hard, making it impossible for the milk to flow. Once this stage has been reached, veterinary attention is required. In extreme cases, the

Brajulste Bitter Sweet (Ellie). One of the handreared pups aged two years old.

teat has to be removed. Tablets can be obtained from the milk to stop your bitch producing milk but the milk that is already present will need to be drained off. This can be done by hand; applying hot flannels to the mother's stomach may also help her to stop producing more milk.

A week or so after her puppies had been removed, Sammy stopped making milk. The tablets from the vet dried up her production whilst my mother expertly handmilked what she had already produced. It is doubtful that Sammy even remembered the puppies she had produced. Five of the pups were sold to nice new homes and we kept a very promising red and white bitch (which is all we were after in the first place!) called Lily. I sincerely hope that none of you reading this have to go through any of this but, if you do, I suppose it is part of life with dogs.

At the end of the day, as I have already said, rearing a litter in the normal way is very rewarding. When you have had to rear a litter with no mother at all, although very, very trying, the feeling of achievement is immeasurable.

Artificial Insemination (AI)

It is due to Arnie's success that I am able to write on this subject. His success in the show ring led to him becoming famous worldwide. Friends of ours who have judged abroad tell us that they have seen many a photo of Arnie on a living room wall! As a consequence of his fame, we started to receive enquiries about obtaining his semen for artificial insemination. People were ringing from Spain, Belgium, Sweden, Australia etc. It was weird to think that all this was happening because of a dog who had been born in a shed in our backyard in a small Derbyshire village, who was now attracting worldwide interest. Up until 3 years ago I didn't have a clue about artificial insemination. Now things are different. When the enquiries started coming I didn't know where to start. I mentioned it to some friends of ours in the breed and they put me in touch with someone who had been through the process in another breed. They told us to contact Tweed House Veterinary Surgery in Leeds. Apparently this is the only vet in the UK who deals with AI. I spoke to Gillian Averis who is not only a vet but a Championship show judge, breeder and exhibitor of Weimaraners. Gillian and the Tweed House staff were very helpful. After booking an appointment, Gillian asked if we had a bitch in season at home. When I asked why, she replied that one would be required as a 'teaser' for Arnie. Unfortunately none of our bitches were in season at the time but luckily Gillian had a Weimaraner we could

1 day old pups, born by AI.

use. (It is preferable if the 'teaser' bitch is of the same breed as the dog but it is not absolutely necessary.)

So off we went - me, Arnie and our old friend Sam, who sadly is no longer with us. Sam was actually more excited about this than me, as he had been in dogs for more than 50 years and never seen anything like it. On arrival at Tweed House we took Arnie through to a small room at the back of the surgery. Gillian's first words were "Wow, he's nice!" I thought she meant me but, alas, it was Arnie she was talking about! I held Arnie on the lead while Gillian bought her Weimaraner bitch through. One of the staff held the bitch whilst I held Arnie behind the rear end of the bitch. I was then instructed to let Arnie go so he could sniff the Weimaraner. What followed was quite comical. Have you ever seen a Stafford trying to mate something which is two and half times as tall as himself?! As Arnie began to recognise the usual smell of a bitch in season, he tried harder to mate her. Several times he was almost standing upright on his hindlegs! Once Arnie started to speed up, Gillian placed her hand underneath the dog. She was holding a rubber sheath, like a condom. This sheath had a test-tube attached to the bottom of it. When Arnie reached maximum thrust, Gillian placed the sheath over his penis. The dog thought he was actually inside the bitch and so began ejaculating. A few moments later, Gillian decided that he had finished and that enough semen had been collected. I had witnessed for the first time how semen was taken for AI. Sam sat there in amazement!

Gillian then placed some semen onto a microscope plate which was placed under a microscope. I was then invited to have a look at Arnie's semen. It was amazing! Millions of baby Arnies swimming in all directions. The semen has to be checked for motility (movement); this is very important because under a certain percentage the semen will not freeze successfully. At 60% motility, four straws are required per insemination. At 50% motility, five straws are required per insemination. Anything less than 50% motility means the semen will not freeze correctly. So when the semen is collected and checked, it is then placed into what are known as 'straws'. The straws are placed in liquid nitrogen containers. They can be kept in these containers indefinitely. Once the semen has been collected and frozen, Tweed House do the rest. Obviously they require an address for the semen to be sent to. This is your responsibility because you will have dealt with the people who will be receiving your dog's semen. One point of interest: Gillian told me that the smaller the dog, the less semen they will produce. So a Great Dane will produce more than a Yorkshire Terrier, for example. On our trips to Tweed House, Arnie produced 8-12 straws on each occasion.

There are 2 ways of inseminating a bitch. One (intra-vaginal) is to insert a tube into the bitch's vulva and then to feed the semen through the tube in the hope that it will find its way

Am Ch Brajulste Fly The Flag - Archie.
Another alternative to exporting dogs would be to make use of AI.

towards the ovaries. This method is not as successful as the second method (intra-uterine). This involves an operation in which the semen is directly implanted into the eggs. So far Arnie has had his semen sent once to America and twice to Australia. The process is not cheap. Having said that, it is usually the person receiving the semen who foots the bill. In 1996, the cost of collection and freezing was £200. To this have to be added the shipping costs and the rental charge for the liquid nitrogen containers. Just getting the semen to America or Australia costs roughly £500. The running cost would therefore be £700-£800, and that's before you've charged your stud fee. As you can see, it's a very expensive exercise.

Countries closer to the UK than America and Australia can be sent fresh, rather than frozen, semen. We have not done this but know people who have. The collection of the semen is the same; the main difference is that it has to be used within 24 hours. The timing obviously has to be spot-on. A correct day for the bitch has to be ascertained and everything else - such as collection, flights etc - is worked around that. Again, this is all handled by Tweed House. Fellow European countries are the usual destination for UK semen. Semen collected fresh and chilled can be sent to Europe and Scandinavia within 36 hours. Since I have never exported fresh sperm, I cannot comment on the cost of this. Tweed House will also store frozen sperm in the liquid nitrogen containers for a cost of £25 per year plus vat.

So in just a few years I've gone from practically never having heard of AI in dogs to becoming quite knowledgeable on the subject. And to think that it is all due to one little Stafford - the most successful Stafford in the history of the breed.

CHAPTER 10

DANGEROUS DOGS ACT 1991 AND THE STAFFORDSHIRE BULL TERRIER

Before I start on this subject let me say that the only reason I decided to cover the Dangerous Dogs Act 1991 is that **I cannot over-emphasise the importance of obtaining a Kennel Club registered puppy**. A Registration Certificate is proof not only that your dog is a registered Staffordshire Bull Terriers but also that its parents and their parents are also registered.

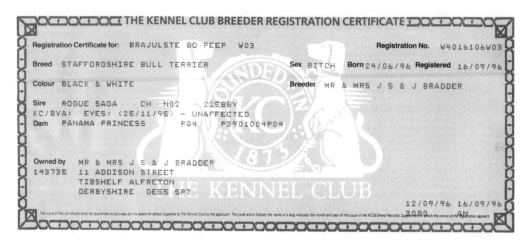

Example of a Kennel Club Registration Certificate.

There are plenty of unregistered dogs out there, readily available. If that's what you want, fine. Just remember, though, that unregistered dogs can never be shown and, more importantly, if you have got yourself an unregistered bitch, you will never be able to use a champion dog at stud (or any registered stud dog, for that matter), because the litters from her will not be eligible for Kennel Club registration either. Therefore you will never improve the quality of your stock.

Now, back to the Dangerous Dogs Act.

After a number of biting incidents, two of them very serious, the Government decided to act very rapidly. They were under pressure from a hysterical press and media and, as a consequence, introduced the most barbaric piece of legislation imaginable: the Dangerous Dogs Act 1991.

Hastily conceived, the Act banned certain breeds from the country and placed cruel restrictions on the Pit Bull Terrier.

The main thrust of the Act was to eliminate the Pit Bull Terrier. Advisors estimated there to be about 10,000 Pit Bull Terriers in the United Kingdom at that time. The Government wanted a programme of mass destruction but opposition from the veterinary profession and the RSPCA resulted in a different approach: enforced castration and spaying, and all dogs to be implanted or tattooed (for identification purposes), registered and insured. All this tied in with the fact that they could only appear in a public place if muzzled and kept on a lead.

As if that wasn't enough for that particular breed, things were made worse with the introduction of the expression 'pit-bull type'. This meant that Staffordshire Bull Terriers were immediately at risk. You could be out with your Stafford and accused at any time by anyone – and I mean 'anyone' – of owning a 'pit-bull-type' dog.

It is at this point that your Registration Certificate becomes absolutely vital.

If your dog is accused of being a 'pit-bull' or 'pit-bull type', it can then be taken away from you and impounded. Then you have to prove to the authorities that you do not own a Pit Bull Terrier. Again, no Registration Certificate – no proof – no chance!

We are fortunate in that, in rural Derbyshire, this does not appear to be a problem. However, in urban areas, particularly in London, the problem is very serious indeed.

Two extreme cases that spring to mind are those of Otis, a Great Dane, and Dempsey, a registered Pit Bull bitch. In the case of Otis, he was seized from his owner's car by police for 'being unmuzzled in a public place'! So now, the inside of your car is deemed to be a public place? An incredible decision with which the Courts evidently agreed. After 5 years of being impounded, Otis was destroyed.

Dempsey, the registered Pit Bull Terrier, was being taken for a walk. Fully muzzled, she began choking. The muzzle was removed to allow her to be sick but she was observed by two police officers. She was seized, accused of being unmuzzled in a public case, found guilty and sentenced to the mandatory death sentence under the Dangerous Dogs Act. After a very long and expensive legal battle the High Court overturned the decision.

There are many, many more cases – needless, inhumane cases that have cost the taxpayer hundreds of thousands of pounds.

I found my own personal experience somewhat unbelievable. We were leaving a Championship show about 3 years ago. As we approached the exit, I observed the two security men on the gate eyeing up Arnie. As I reached into my pocket for the removal order, I heard one say to the other, "Is that one of them Pit Bulls?" I gave him the removal order, looked at him in amazement, shook my head and walked off. I cannot print what was going through my mind. They were looking at a Champion Staffordshire Bull Terrier – in fact the future Breed Record Holder. They didn't have a clue, not a clue. And these are the people with the powers of seizure, the people in the know. What an absolute disgrace!

However, after intense campaigning, especially by people directly affected by the Dangerous Dogs Act, Roger Gale's MP's Dangerous Dogs Act Amendment Bill finally passed through Parliament in March 1997 after a number of earlier attempts. The Amendment finally became law in June 1997. The crux of the Amendment is that the death sentence is no longer mandatory. Thank God!

The following pages contain details of the Dangerous Dogs Act for your information. To obtain your own copy (and any subsequent amendments) apply to The Stationery Office Ltd (formerly known as HMSO), St Crispins, Duke Street, Norwich NR3 1GN (tel 0870 600 5522).

The Act should be read carefully, paying particular attention to *Section 3: Keeping Dogs Under Proper Control* (pages 112-113). Staffordshire Bull Terrier owners still, as always, have to be extremely careful.

ELIZABETH II   c. 30

Dangerous Dogs Act 1989

1989 CHAPTER 30

An Act to extend the powers available to a court on a complaint under section 2 of the Dogs Act 1871 together with additional rights of appeal and enhanced penalties.   [27th July 1989]

BE IT ENACTED by the Queen's most Excellent Majesty, by and with the advice and consent of the Lords Spiritual and Temporal, and Commons, in this present Parliament assembled, and by the authority of the same, as follows:—

1.—(1) Where a magistrates' court makes an order under section 2 of the Dogs Act 1871 directing a dog to be destroyed it may also—

    (a) appoint a person to undertake its destruction and require any person having custody of the dog to deliver it up for that purpose; and

    (b) if it thinks fit, make an order disqualifying the owner for having custody of a dog for such period as is specified in the order.

Additional powers of court on complaint about dangerous dog.
1871 c. 56.

(2) An appeal shall lie to the Crown Court against any order under section 2 of that Act or under subsection (1) above; and, unless the owner of a dog which is ordered to be delivered up and destroyed gives notice to the court that made the order that he does not intend to appeal against it, the dog shall not be destroyed pursuant to the order—

    (a) until the end of the period within which notice of appeal to the Crown Court against the order can be given; and

    (b) if notice of appeal is given within that period, until the appeal is determined or withdrawn.

(3) Any person who fails to comply with an order under section 2 of the said Act of 1871 to keep a dog under proper control or to deliver a dog up for destruction as required by an order under subsection (1)(a) above is guilty of an offence and liable on summary conviction to a fine not exceeding level 3 on the standard scale and the court may, in addition, make an order disqualifying him for having custody of a dog for such period as is specified in the order.

2   c. **30**   *Dangerous Dogs Act 1989*

(4) A person who is disqualified for having custody of a dog by virtue of an order made under subsection (1)(b) or (3) above may, at any time after the end of the period of one year beginning with the date of the order, apply to the court that made it (or any magistrates' court acting for the same petty sessions area as that court) for a direction terminating the disqualification.

(5) On an application under subsection (4) above the court may—

(a) having regard to the applicant's character, his conduct since the disqualification was imposed and any other circumstances of the case, grant or refuse the application; and

(b) order the applicant to pay all or any part of the costs of the application;

and where an application in respect of an order is refused no further application in respect of that order shall be entertained if made before the end of the period of one year beginning with the date of the refusal.

(6) Any person who has custody of a dog in contravention of an order made under subsection (1)(b) or (3) above is guilty of an offence and liable on summary conviction to a fine not exceeding level 5 on the standard scale.

(7) This section shall apply to Scotland subject to the following adaptations—

(a) in subsection (1) for the words "magistrates' court" there shall be substituted the words "court of summary jurisdiction";

(b) in subsection (2)—

(i) for the words "shall lie to the Crown Court" there shall be substituted the words "may be made to the High Court within a period of 7 days commencing with the date of the order";

(ii) for paragraph (a) there shall be substituted—

"(a) until the end of the said period of 7 days; and";

(c) in subsection (4) the words "(or any magistrates' court acting for the same petty sessions area as that court)" shall be omitted.

Short title, consequential amendment and repeals, commencement and extent.
1871 c. 56.
1975 c. 21.

2.—(1) This Act may be cited as the Dangerous Dogs Act 1989.

(2) In section 5 of the Dogs Act 1871 for the definition of "court of summary jurisdiction" there shall be substituted—

" "court of summary jurisdiction" as regards Scotland has the same meaning as in section 462 of the Criminal Procedure (Scotland) Act 1975."

(3) The following provisions (which are superseded by this Act or otherwise spent) are hereby repealed—

(a) in the Dogs Act 1871, in section 2, the words from "and any person failing to comply" onwards, section 4 and in section 6 the words "in the eighteenth section of the Metropolitan Streets Act 1867, or";

1938 c. 21.

(b) the Dogs (Amendment) Act 1938.

(4) This Act shall come into force at the end of the period of one month beginning with the day on which it is passed and does not affect the said Acts of 1871 and 1938 in relation to any complaint made before the coming into force of this Act.

(5) This Act does not extend to Northern Ireland.

PRINTED IN THE UNITED KINGDOM BY PAUL FREEMAN
Controller and Chief Executive of Her Majesty's Stationery Office and
Queen's Printer of Acts of Parliament.

Dangerous Dogs Act 1991

CHAPTER 65

ARRANGEMENT OF SECTIONS

ELIZABETH II   c. **65**

Dangerous Dogs Act 1991

1991 CHAPTER 65

An Act to prohibit persons from having in their possession or custody dogs belonging to types bred for fighting; to impose restrictions in respect of such dogs pending the coming into force of the prohibition; to enable restrictions to be imposed in relation to other types of dog which present a serious danger to the public; to make further provision for securing that dogs are kept under proper control; and for connected purposes.

[25th July 1991]

B E IT ENACTED by the Queen's most Excellent Majesty, by and with the advice and consent of the Lords Spiritual and Temporal, and Commons, in this present Parliament assembled, and by the authority of the same, as follows:—

1.—(1) This section applies to— *Dogs bred for fighting.*

    (a) any dog of the type known as the pit bull terrier;

    (b) any dog of the type known as the Japanese tosa; and

    (c) any dog of any type designated for the purposes of this section by an order of the Secretary of State, being a type appearing to him to be bred for fighting or to have the characteristics of a type bred for that purpose.

(2) No person shall—

    (a) breed, or breed from, a dog to which this section applies;

    (b) sell or exchange such a dog or offer, advertise or expose such a dog for sale or exchange;

    (c) make or offer to make a gift of such a dog or advertise or expose such a dog as a gift;

    (d) allow such a dog of which he is the owner or of which he is for the time being in charge to be in a public place without being muzzled and kept on a lead; or

(e) abandon such a dog of which he is the owner or, being the owner or for the time being in charge of such a dog, allow it to stray.

(3) After such day as the Secretary of State may by order appoint for the purposes of this subsection no person shall have any dog to which this section applies in his possession or custody except—

(a) in pursuance of the power of seizure conferred by the subsequent provisions of this Act; or

(b) in accordance with an order for its destruction made under those provisions;

but the Secretary of State shall by order make a scheme for the payment to the owners of such dogs who arrange for them to be destroyed before that day of sums specified in or determined under the scheme in respect of those dogs and the cost of their destruction.

(4) Subsection (2)(b) and (c) above shall not make unlawful anything done with a view to the dog in question being removed from the United Kingdom before the day appointed under subsection (3) above.

(5) The Secretary of State may by order provide that the prohibition in subsection (3) above shall not apply in such cases and subject to compliance with such conditions as are specified in the order and any such provision may take the form of a scheme of exemption containing such arrangements (including provision for the payment of charges or fees) as he thinks appropriate.

(6) A scheme under subsection (3) or (5) above may provide for specified functions under the scheme to be discharged by such persons or bodies as the Secretary of State thinks appropriate.

(7) Any person who contravenes this section is guilty of an offence and liable on summary conviction to imprisonment for a term not exceeding six months or a fine not exceeding level 5 on the standard scale or both except that a person who publishes an advertisement in contravention of subsection (2)(b) or (c)—

(a) shall not on being convicted be liable to imprisonment if he shows that he published the advertisement to the order of someone else and did not himself devise it; and

(b) shall not be convicted if, in addition, he shows that he did not know and had no reasonable cause to suspect that it related to a dog to which this section applies.

(8) An order under subsection (1)(c) above adding dogs of any type to those to which this section applies may provide that subsections (3) and (4) above shall apply in relation to those dogs with the substitution for the day appointed under subsection (3) of a later day specified in the order.

(9) The power to make orders under this section shall be exercisable by statutory instrument which, in the case of an order under subsection (1) or (5) or an order containing a scheme under subsection (3), shall be subject to annulment in pursuance of a resolution of either House of Parliament.

2.—(1) If it appears to the Secretary of State that dogs of any type to which section 1 above does not apply present a serious danger to the public he may by order impose in relation to dogs of that type restrictions corresponding, with such modifications, if any, as he thinks appropriate, to all or any of those in subsection (2)(d) and (e) of that section.

Other specially dangerous dogs.

(2) An order under this section may provide for exceptions from any restriction imposed by the order in such cases and subject to compliance with such conditions as are specified in the order.

(3) An order under this section may contain such supplementary or transitional provisions as the Secretary of State thinks necessary or expedient and may create offences punishable on summary conviction with imprisonment for a term not exceeding six months or a fine not exceeding level 5 on the standard scale or both.

(4) In determining whether to make an order under this section in relation to dogs of any type and, if so, what the provisions of the order should be, the Secretary of State shall consult with such persons or bodies as appear to him to have relevant knowledge or experience, including a body concerned with animal welfare, a body concerned with veterinary science and practice and a body concerned with breeds of dogs.

(5) The power to make an order under this section shall be exercisable by statutory instrument and no such order shall be made unless a draft of it has been laid before and approved by a resolution of each House of Parliament.

3.—(1) If a dog is dangerously out of control in a public place—

(a) the owner; and

(b) if different, the person for the time being in charge of the dog,

is guilty of an offence, or, if the dog while so out of control injures any person, an aggravated offence, under this subsection.

Keeping dogs under proper control.

(2) In proceedings for an offence under subsection (1) above against a person who is the owner of a dog but was not at the material time in charge of it, it shall be a defence for the accused to prove that the dog was at the material time in the charge of a person whom he reasonably believed to be a fit and proper person to be in charge of it.

(3) If the owner or, if different, the person for the time being in charge of a dog allows it to enter a place which is not a public place but where it is not permitted to be and while it is there—

(a) it injures any person; or

(b) there are grounds for reasonable apprehension that it will do so,

he is guilty of an offence, or, if the dog injures any person, an aggravated offence, under this subsection.

(4) A person guilty of an offence under subsection (1) or (3) above other than an aggravated offence is liable on summary conviction to imprisonment for a term not exceeding six months or a fine not exceeding level 5 on the standard scale or both; and a person guilty of an aggravated offence under either of those subsections is liable—

(a) on summary conviction, to imprisonment for a term not exceeding six months or a fine not exceeding the statutory maximum or both;

4   c. **65**   *Dangerous Dogs Act 1991*

(b) on conviction on indictment, to imprisonment for a term not exceeding two years or a fine or both.

1871 c.56.

(5) It is hereby declared for the avoidance of doubt that an order under section 2 of the Dogs Act 1871 (order on complaint that dog is dangerous and not kept under proper control)—

(a) may be made whether or not the dog is shown to have injured any person; and

(b) may specify the measures to be taken for keeping the dog under proper control, whether by muzzling, keeping on a lead, excluding it from specified places or otherwise.

(6) If it appears to a court on a complaint under section 2 of the said Act of 1871 that the dog to which the complaint relates is a male and would be less dangerous if neutered the court may under that section make an order requiring it to be neutered.

1989 c. 30.

(7) The reference in section 1(3) of the Dangerous Dogs Act 1989 (penalties) to failing to comply with an order under section 2 of the said Act of 1871 to keep a dog under proper control shall include a reference to failing to comply with any other order made under that section; but no order shall be made under that section by virtue of subsection (6) above where the matters complained of arose before the coming into force of that subsection.

Destruction and disqualification orders.

4.—(1) Where a person is convicted of an offence under section 1 or 3(1) or (3) above or of an offence under an order made under section 2 above the court—

(a) may order the destruction of any dog in respect of which the offence was committed and shall do so in the case of an offence under section 1 or an aggravated offence under section 3(1) or (3) above; and

(b) may order the offender to be disqualified, for such period as the court thinks fit, for having custody of a dog.

(2) Where a court makes an order under subsection (1)(a) above for the destruction of a dog owned by a person other than the offender, then, unless the order is one that the court is required to make, the owner may appeal to the Crown Court against the order.

(3) A dog shall not be destroyed pursuant to an order under subsection (1)(a) above—

(a) until the end of the period for giving notice of appeal against the conviction or, where the order was not one which the court was required to make, against the order; and

(b) if notice of appeal is given within that period, until the appeal is determined or withdrawn,

unless the offender and, in a case to which subsection (2) above applies, the owner of the dog give notice to the court that made the order that there is to be no appeal.

(4) Where a court makes an order under subsection (1)(a) above it may—

(a) appoint a person to undertake the destruction of the dog and require any person having custody of it to deliver it up for that purpose; and

(b) order the offender to pay such sum as the court may determine to be the reasonable expenses of destroying the dog and of keeping it pending its destruction.

(5) Any sum ordered to be paid under subsection (4)(b) above shall be treated for the purposes of enforcement as if it were a fine imposed on conviction.

(6) Any person who is disqualified for having custody of a dog by virtue of an order under subsection (1)(b) above may, at any time after the end of the period of one year beginning with the date of the order, apply to the court that made it (or a magistrates' court acting for the same petty sessions area as that court) for a direction terminating the disqualification.

(7) On an application under subsection (6) above the court may—

(a) having regard to the applicant's character, his conduct since the disqualification was imposed and any other circumstances of the case, grant or refuse the application; and

(b) order the applicant to pay all or any part of the costs of the application;

and where an application in respect of an order is refused no further application in respect of that order shall be entertained if made before the end of the period of one year beginning with the date of the refusal.

(8) Any person who—

(a) has custody of a dog in contravention of an order under subsection (1)(b) above; or

(b) fails to comply with a requirement imposed on him under subsection (4)(a) above,

is guilty of an offence and liable on summary conviction to a fine not exceeding level 5 on the standard scale.

(9) In the application of this section to Scotland—

(a) in subsection (2) for the words "Crown Court against the order" there shall be substituted the words "High Court of Justiciary against the order within the period of seven days beginning with the date of the order";

(b) for subsection (3)(a) there shall be substituted—

"(a) until the end of the period of seven days beginning with the date of the order";

(c) for subsection (5) there shall be substituted—

"(5) Section 411 of the Criminal Procedure (Scotland) Act 1975 shall apply in relation to the recovery of sums ordered to be paid under subsection (4)(b) above as it applies to fines ordered to be recovered by civil diligence in pursuance of Part II of that Act."; and   1975 c. 21.

(d) in subsection (6) the words "(or a magistrates' court acting for the same petty sessions area as that court)" shall be omitted.

5.—(1) A constable or an officer of a local authority authorised by it to exercise the powers conferred by this subsection may seize—   Seizure, entry of premises and evidence.

(a) any dog which appears to him to be a dog to which section 1 above applies and which is in a public place—

(i) after the time when possession or custody of it has become unlawful by virtue of that section; or

(ii) before that time, without being muzzled and kept on a lead;

(b) any dog in a public place which appears to him to be a dog to which an order under section 2 above applies and in respect of which an offence against the order has been or is being committed; and

(c) any dog in a public place (whether or not one to which that section or such an order applies) which appears to him to be dangerously out of control.

(2) If a justice of the peace is satisfied by information on oath, or in Scotland a justice of the peace or sheriff is satisfied by evidence on oath, that there are reasonable grounds for believing—

(a) that an offence under any provision of this Act or of an order under section 2 above is being or has been committed; or

(b) that evidence of the commission of any such offence is to be found,

on any premises he may issue a warrant authorising a constable to enter those premises (using such force as is reasonably necessary) and to search them and seize any dog or other thing found there which is evidence of the commission of such an offence.

(3) A warrant issued under this section in Scotland shall be authority for opening lockfast places and may authorise persons named in the warrant to accompany a constable who is executing it.

(4) Where a dog is seized under subsection (1) or (2) above and it appears to a justice of the peace, or in Scotland a justice of the peace or sheriff, that no person has been or is to be prosecuted for an offence under this Act or an order under section 2 above in respect of that dog (whether because the owner cannot be found or for any other reason) he may order the destruction of the dog and shall do so if it is one to which section 1 above applies.

(5) If in any proceedings it is alleged by the prosecution that a dog is one to which section 1 or an order under section 2 above applies it shall be presumed that it is such a dog unless the contrary is shown by the accused by such evidence as the court considers sufficient; and the accused shall not be permitted to adduce such evidence unless he has given the prosecution notice of his intention to do so not later than the fourteenth day before that on which the evidence is to be adduced.

Dogs owned by young persons.

6. Where a dog is owned by a person who is less than sixteen years old any reference to its owner in section 1(2)(d) or (e) or 3 above shall include a reference to the head of the household, if any, of which that person is a member or, in Scotland, to the person who has his actual care and control.

Muzzling and leads.

7.—(1) In this Act—

(a) references to a dog being muzzled are to its being securely fitted with a muzzle sufficient to prevent it biting any person; and

(b) references to its being kept on a lead are to its being securely held on a lead by a person who is not less than sixteen years old.

(2) If the Secretary of State thinks it desirable to do so he may by order prescribe the kind of muzzle or lead to be used for the purpose of complying, in the case of a dog of any type, with section 1 or an order under section 2 above; and if a muzzle or lead of a particular kind is for the time being prescribed in relation to any type of dog the references in subsection (1) above to a muzzle or lead shall, in relation to any dog of that type, be construed as references to a muzzle or lead of that kind.

(3) The power to make an order under subsection (2) above shall be exercisable by statutory instrument subject to annulment in pursuance of a resolution of either House of Parliament.

8. An Order in Council under paragraph 1(1)(b) of Schedule 1 to the Northern Ireland Act 1974 (legislation for Northern Ireland in the interim period) which states that it is made only for purposes corresponding to the purposes of this Act—

Power to make corresponding provision for Northern Ireland.
1974 c. 28.

> (a) shall not be subject to paragraph 1(4) and (5) of that Schedule (affirmative resolution of both Houses of Parliament); but
>
> (b) shall be subject to annulment in pursuance of a resolution of either House.

9. Any expenses incurred by the Secretary of State in consequence of this Act shall be paid out of money provided by Parliament.

Expenses.

10.—(1) This Act may be cited as the Dangerous Dogs Act 1991.

(2) In this Act—

Short title, interpretation, commencement and extent.

> "advertisement" includes any means of bringing a matter to the attention of the public and "advertise" shall be construed accordingly;
>
> "public place" means any street, road or other place (whether or not enclosed) to which the public have or are permitted to have access whether for payment or otherwise and includes the common parts of a building containing two or more separate dwellings.

(3) For the purposes of this Act a dog shall be regarded as dangerously out of control on any occasion on which there are grounds for reasonable apprehension that it will injure any person, whether or not it actually does so, but references to a dog injuring a person or there being grounds for reasonable apprehension that it will do so do not include references to any case in which the dog is being used for a lawful purpose by a constable or a person in the service of the Crown.

(4) Except for section 8, this Act shall not come into force until such day as the Secretary of State may appoint by an order made by statutory instrument and different days may be appointed for different provisions or different purposes.

(5) Except for section 8, this Act does not extend to Northern Ireland.

Dangerous Dogs (Amendment) Act 1997

CHAPTER 53

ARRANGEMENT OF SECTIONS

ELIZABETH II   c. 53

Dangerous Dogs (Amendment) Act 1997

1997 CHAPTER 53

An Act to amend the Dangerous Dogs Act 1991; and for connected purposes.   [21st March 1997]

BE IT ENACTED by the Queen's most Excellent Majesty, by and with the advice and consent of the Lords Spiritual and Temporal, and Commons, in this present Parliament assembled, and by the authority of the same, as follows:—

1.—(1) In paragraph (a) of subsection (1) of section 4 (destruction and disqualification orders) of the Dangerous Dogs Act 1991 ("the 1991 Act"), after the words "committed and" there shall be inserted the words ", subject to subsection (1A) below,". Destruction orders.
1991 c. 65.

(2) After that subsection there shall be inserted the following subsection—

"(1A) Nothing in subsection (1)(a) above shall require the court to order the destruction of a dog if the court is satisfied—

(a) that the dog would not constitute a danger to public safety; and

(b) where the dog was born before 30th November 1991 and is subject to the prohibition in section 1(3) above, that there is a good reason why the dog has not been exempted from that prohibition."

(3) In subsection (2) of that section, the words "then, unless the order is one that the court is required to make" shall cease to have effect.

(4) In subsection (3)(a) of that section, the words ", where the order was not one that the court was required to make" shall cease to have effect.

Contingent
destruction
orders.

2. After section 4 of the 1991 Act there shall be inserted the following section—

"Contingent
destruction
orders.

4A.—(1) Where—

(a) a person is convicted of an offence under section 1 above or an aggravated offence under section 3(1) or (3) above;

(b) the court does not order the destruction of the dog under section 4(1)(a) above; and

(c) in the case of an offence under section 1 above, the dog is subject to the prohibition in section 1(3) above,

the court shall order that, unless the dog is exempted from that prohibition within the requisite period, the dog shall be destroyed.

(2) Where an order is made under subsection (1) above in respect of a dog, and the dog is not exempted from the prohibition in section 1(3) above within the requisite period, the court may extend that period.

(3) Subject to subsection (2) above, the requisite period for the purposes of such an order is the period of two months beginning with the date of the order.

(4) Where a person is convicted of an offence under section 3(1) or (3) above, the court may order that, unless the owner of the dog keeps it under proper control, the dog shall be destroyed.

(5) An order under subsection (4) above—

(a) may specify the measures to be taken for keeping the dog under proper control, whether by muzzling, keeping on a lead, excluding it from specified places or otherwise; and

(b) if it appears to the court that the dog is a male and would be less dangerous if neutered, may require it to be neutered.

(6) Subsections (2) to (4) of section 4 above shall apply in relation to an order under subsection (1) or (4) above as they apply in relation to an order under subsection (1)(a) of that section."

Destruction
orders otherwise
than on a
conviction.

3.—(1) After section 4A of the 1991 Act there shall be inserted the following section—

"Destruction
orders otherwise
than on a
conviction.

4B.—(1) Where a dog is seized under section 5(1) or (2) below and it appears to a justice of the peace, or in Scotland a justice of the peace or sheriff—

(a) that no person has been or is to be prosecuted for an offence under this Act or an order under section 2 above in respect of that dog (whether because the owner cannot be found or for any other reason); or

(b) that the dog cannot be released into the custody or possession of its owner without the owner contravening the prohibition in section 1(3) above,

he may order the destruction of the dog and, subject to subsection (2) below, shall do so if it is one to which section 1 above applies.

(2) Nothing in subsection (1)(b) above shall require the justice or sheriff to order the destruction of a dog if he is satisfied—

    (a) that the dog would not constitute a danger to public safety; and

    (b) where the dog was born before 30th November 1991 and is subject to the prohibition in section 1(3) above, that there is a good reason why the dog has not been exempted from that prohibition.

(3) Where in a case falling within subsection (1)(b) above the justice or sheriff does not order the destruction of the dog, he shall order that, unless the dog is exempted from the prohibition in section 1(3) above within the requisite period, the dog shall be destroyed.

(4) Subsections (2) to (4) of section 4 above shall apply in relation to an order under subsection (1)(b) or (3) above as they apply in relation to an order under subsection (1)(a) of that section.

(5) Subsections (2) and (3) of section 4A above shall apply in relation to an order under subsection (3) above as they apply in relation to an order under subsection (1) of that section, except that the reference to the court in subsection (2) of that section shall be construed as a reference to the justice or sheriff."

(2) In section 5 of the 1991 Act (seizure, entry of premises and evidence), subsection (4) (which is superseded by this section) shall cease to have effect.

4.—(1) Where an order is made under section 4A(1) or 4B(3) of the 1991 Act, Part III of the Dangerous Dogs Compensation and Exemption Schemes Order 1991 (exemption scheme) shall have effect as if—

Extended application of 1991 Order.
S.I. 1991/1744.

    (a) any reference to the appointed day were a reference to the end of the requisite period within the meaning of section 4A or, as the case may be, section 4B of the 1991 Act;

    (b) paragraph (a) of Article 4 and Article 6 were omitted; and

    (c) the fee payable to the Agency under Article 9 were a fee of such amount as the Secretary of State may by order prescribe.

(2) The power to make an order under this section shall be exercisable by statutory instrument which shall be subject to annulment in pursuance of a resolution of either House of Parliament.

4   c. **53**   *Dangerous Dogs (Amendment) Act 1997*

Transitional
provisions.

5.—(1) This Act shall apply in relation to cases where proceedings have been instituted before, as well as after, the commencement of this Act.

(2) In a case where, before the commencement of this Act—

(a) the court has ordered the destruction of a dog in respect of which an offence under section 1, or an aggravated offence under section 3(1) or (3), of the 1991 Act has been committed, but

(b) the dog has not been destroyed,

that destruction order shall cease to have effect and the case shall be remitted to the court for reconsideration.

(3) Where a case is so remitted, the court may make any order in respect of the dog which it would have power to make if the person in question had been convicted of the offence after the commencement of this Act.

Short title,
commencement
and extent.

6.—(1) This Act may be cited as the Dangerous Dogs (Amendment) Act 1997.

(2) This Act does not extend to Northern Ireland.

(3) This Act shall come into force on such day as the Secretary of State may by order made by statutory instrument appoint.

Printed in the UK by The Stationery Office Limited
under the authority and superintendence of Peter Macdonald, Controller of
Her Majesty's Stationery Office and Queen's Printer of Acts of Parliament

APPENDIX A

CH DOMINO FLASHY LAD
(BREED RECORD HOLDER)

The following are extracts from articles written about our top-winning champion Ch Domino Flashy Lad (known to his friends as Arnie) for the NISBTC magazine:

Arnie (Ch Domino Flashy Lad) was born along with his four litter brothers on the 24 July 1991. At the age of 6 weeks they were all very even. Two highly acclaimed Staffordshire Bull Terrier Championship Show judges came to look at the litter. They were both of the same opinion: there was nothing to choose between them. Consequently, Arnie was sold at the age of 6$^{1}/_{2}$ weeks.

What a bunch! Arnie's litter.

Sarah Whittaker, brought him back to show us when he was 12 weeks old. Julie and I looked at each other in disbelief. At this age, his head shape had completely altered: he looked exactly like his father, Ch Rogue Saga. We had sold the wrong puppy! We knew from that day that Arnie was a potential champion. During 1992 Sarah showed him a few times but never with the seriousness or belief that the dog demanded.

At the NCSBTC Championship Show 1992 a well known Staffordshire Bull Terrier enthusiast spoke to Sarah's father, Jim, stating the potential of the dog and the need for him to be campaigned properly. Jim agreed and this is where I came into the equation; as well as having bred the dog, I would

The future Breed Record Holder at 6 weeks old.

now show him. Over the coming months we got to know Sarah's parents Jim and Maureen very well. We hit it off with them from the word go. We got on like a house on fire. They both quickly became our friends.

We came to an agreement whereby Jim paid for all the entries for the shows and I paid for the petrol. When it came to Arnie's stud work, a 50/50 split was agreed. If a show was at the

Head study of Arnie.

At the Welsh Kennel Club (Arnie's 8th CC).

weekend, I'd nip down to Jim's say on the Wednesday, pick Arnie up, then he'd stay at our place so that I could exercise him, bath him and generally get him in what I considered to be good show condition. After the show, Arnie was returned to the Whittaker household whereon we indulged in many a glass of fine malt whiskey, more often than not far too many, for Jim was something of a connoisseur of the stuff.

A few days before the EASBTC Open Show in February 1994 I picked the dog up as usual. He went on to BIS under judge Jim Holmes. With this show being so close to Crufts and Jim due in hospital for a hip replacement operation it was decided that Arnie would stay with us until after Crufts; in fact until Jim had had his operation and was fit enough again to cope with a young, boisterous Stafford. Tragically, that day never came. On the day before Crufts, Sarah telephoned. The news was devastating. Having had his hip operation 4 days previously, Jim suffered a massive heart attack whist still in hospital recuperating. That was that. No warning. No second chance. Jim had died. To say that we were devastated is an understatement. We cried all day. I did not want then to take the dog to Crufts. I was so upset. Jim's wife, Maureen, told us we must go: Jim wouldn't have wanted it any other way. We went, and Arnie won his class.

The day after the show, Maureen telephoned, asking us to go down. She had something to tell us. Immediately, I thought I would not be able to show Arnie any more. How wrong I was. When we got there, the house was full of other members of the family. Everybody was understandably devastated. The shock of losing Jim was unbearable. Maureen asked us if we would have Arnie back for good as now she could not possibly cope with him. She assured us

Ch Domino Flashy Lad.

that it would have been what Jim would have wanted. So we had him back, albeit in terrible and very sad circumstances. The saddest part of all was that Jim never saw his dog become a champion, a dream we had all shared since Arnie was a puppy. How proud he would have been. We still go down to Maureen's on a regular basis but writing this, almost a year after Jim's death, it is still very, very difficult to come to terms with what happened.

On that day in March 1994 we lost a very dear friend, a man with a huge heart who would have done anything for us. I just hope that somewhere up there Jim is watching and knows what a stir Arnie is causing.

Manchester 1995.

On a brighter note, we've campaigned Arnie all over the place. He's won CCs in England, Ireland, Scotland and Wales **All Arnie's wins and achievements are dedicated to the memory of Jim Whittaker, 'Our Friend'.**

Steve now updates the story. As the 1995 show season approached, we wondered if Arnie could carry on winning CCs or if that, as they say, was that. We didn't have to wait long to find out. Manchester at the G Mex under Jack Miller, first Championship show of the year and Arnie won his 15th CC with BOB and finished third in the Group. Another high point at this show for us was that Best Puppy was won by one of Arnie's daughters, Alan and Pauline Raymond's Rockstaff Gipsy Queen. Winning the CC

Record breaking day at the Notts and Derby District SBT Club Championship Show 1995.

and BOB at Crufts and representing our breed in the big ring surely, we thought, could not be topped but a fortnight later it was.

CC no. 17 with BOB and then later BIS at The National Terrier. That day will stay with me for the rest of my life. The first Stafford ever to achieve this accolade. We were so proud for everyone in Staffords. What a great day for us all!

More CCs then followed at Birmingham National, Bath, Blackpool (where he equalled Ch Constones Yer Man's record) and then the Notts and Derby Championship Show, where he finally took the record under Sarah Hemstock. This proved a little too much to handle for myself and Julie. We both broke down and cried unashamedly. All I could think about was the dog and that he'd done it all on his own – well, perhaps with a little help from us. The support from both our families has been second to none, especially when the back-stabbing and everything that goes with having a top-winning dog almost got the better of us. Believe me, at one stage Julie was

Celebrating after Arnie's record 21st CC.

getting so upset that people were changing towards us, I nearly threw the towel in.

The first person to congratulate us on breaking the CC record was, contrary to popular belief, Clare Lee, who was I think genuinely chuffed for us and what we had achieved. Let's face it, 4 years earlier I didn't even know how to stand a dog, never mind have the Breed Record Holder. I suppose in some respects I'm different in that I don't care if the dog wins or loses. If he wins, brilliant – if he loses, who cares?

Arnie went on to win a total of 28 Challenge Certificates and 12 Reserve CCS. He's done his bit for himself, he's done his bit for us but, above all, he's done his bit for Staffords.

What a day for Staffords!
The only Stafford in history to win Best in Show at The National Terrier Club Championship Show in 1995.
Judge: Ann Roslin-Williams.

Arnie's wins

Challenge Certificates

Midland Counties 1993; Manchester 1994; West of England Ladies Kennel Society 1994; Birmingham National 1994; Windsor 1994; Leeds 1994; Bournemouth 1994; Welsh Kennel Club 1994; Scottish Kennel Club 1994; Darlington 1994; Belfast 1994; Western SBT Society 1994; Midland Counties 1994; East Midlands SBTC 1994; Manchester 1995; Crufts 1995; National Terrier 1995; Birmingham National 1995; Bath 1995; Blackpool 1995; Notts & Derby District SBT Club 1995; Scottish Kennel Club 1995; Belfast 1995; Driffield 1995; Western SBT Club 1995; Belfast 1996; Southern Counties SBT Society 1996; Ladies Kennel Association 1996.

Reserve Challenge Certificates

East of England 1993; East Midlands 1993; National Terrier 1994; East of England 1994; Staffordshire Bull Terrier Club 1994; Ladies Kennel Association 1994; Southern Counties Canine Association 1995; Crufts 1996; Bath 1996; Northern Counties SBT Club 1996; East Midlands SBT Club 1996; Western SBT Society 1998.

Terrier Groups

Reserve Best Terrier Windsor 1994
Reserve Best Terrier Midland Counties 1994
Best Terrier and Best in Show National Terrier 1995
Reserve Best Terrier Belfast 1996

Best Terrier Bournemouth 1994
Terrier Group 3 Manchester 1995
Reserve Best Terrier SKC 1995

PEDIGREE OF CH DOMINO FLASHY LAD

Parents	Grandparents	G-Grandparents	G-G-Grandparents	G-G-G-Grandparents
Ch Rogue Saga	Ch Lancstaff Sparbu Saga	Ch The Malaser Mauler	Ch Jokartan Royal Tan	Ch Jolhem Ringmaster
				Brodiffe Bountiful
			Pitmax Brazen Lady	Ch Swinten Sky Scraper
				Lady Red Samba
		Jaunty Jane of Lancstaff	Ch Red Rum	Vencristo Domino
				Vencristo Amber
			Komische Kiwi	Ch Hurricane of Judael
				Jinnie Arenskaya
	Rogue Goddess (JW)	Rogue Duke	Goldwyn Golden Lad	Ch Red Rum
				Star Prize
			Lady of Stony	Snow Soldier
				Bess of Stony
		Snow Goddess	Snow Soldier	Chapultapec Boy
				Trawwall Breeders Dream
			Atlanta Greek Goddess	Barush Brigands Stafl
				Zepplin Fighter
Panama Princess	Elvinor Pied Piper	Ch Teutonic Warrior	Ashstock Wild Colonial Boy	Ch Montbell Barbarossa
				Ashstock Belle Buttons
			Regal Princess	Ashstock Red Rebel
				Pride of Monkswood
		Elvinor Isobella	Whitstaff the Red Rebel of Elvinor	Sunrise Fireflash
				Pitmax Miss Prim
			Elvinor Electra	Brenstaff Double Top
				Ashmoss Rosina of Elvinor
	Little Churub	Rockies Pride	Barush Comet King	Lizsara Chieftian Warrior
				Border Donna of Barush
			Normandy Nett	Battlement Major
				Birchstaff Eve of Christmas
		Holy of Eve	Barush Redstaff	Lizsara Chieftian WArrior
				Border Donna of Barush
			Birchstaff Eve of Christmas	Ch Kandony Brindle Ben
				Rowestaff Bonny Lass

RULES FOR A TYPICAL DOG FIGHT
(19TH CENTURY)

Rules

1   To be a fair fight .... yards from scratch.

2   Both dogs to be tested before and after fighting if required.

3   Both dogs to be shown fair to the scratch and washed at their own corners.

4   Both seconds to deliver the dogs fair from the corner and not leave until the dogs commence fighting.

5   A referee to be chosen in the pit; one minute time to be allowed between every fair go away; fifty seconds allowed for sponging; and at the expiration of that time the timekeeper shall call "Make Ready" and as soon as the minute is expired the dogs to be delivered and the dog refusing or stopping on the way to be the loser.

6   Should either second pick up his dog in a mistake, he shall put it down immediately by order of the referee or the money to be forfeited.

7   Should anything pernicious be found on either dog before or after fighting in the pit, the backers of the dog so found to forfeit and the person holding the battle money to give it up immediately when called upon to do so.

8   Referee to be chosen in the pit before fighting whose decision in all cases to be final.

9   Either dog exceeding the stipulated weight on the day of weighing to forfeit money deposited.

10   In any case of a dog being declared dead by the referee, the living dog shall remain at him for 10 minutes when he shall be taken to his corner if it be his turn to scratch or if it be the dead dog's turn the fight shall be at an end by order of the referee.

11   In any case of Police interference, the Referee to name the next place and time of fighting, on the same day if possible and day by day until it be decided, but if no Referee be chosen, the Stakeholder to name the next place and time; but if a Referee has been chosen and then refuses to name the next place and time of fighting or goes away after being disturbed, then the power of choosing the next time and place be left with the Stakeholder and a fresh Referee to be chosen in the pit and the power of the former one be entirely gone.

12   In the case of Police interference and the dogs have commenced fighting they will not be required to weigh any more. but if they have not commenced fighting they will have to weigh day by day at .... lb, until decided at the time and place named by the Referee, or if he refuses to go away, then the Stakeholder has to name the time and place.

13   The seconder of either dog is upon no consideration to call his adversary's dog by name while in the pit, nor to use anything whatever in his hands with which to call his dog off.

14   To toss up the night before fighting for the place of fighting between the hours of .... and .... o' clock at the house where the last deposit is made.

15   The above stakes are not to be given up until fairly won, or lost by a fight, unless either party break the above agreement.

16   All deposits to be made between the hours of .... and .... o' clock at night.

17   Either party not following up or breaking the above agreement to forfeit the money down.

....

....

Witnesses   ....   Signed......................................

            ....

USEFUL ADDRESSES

Staffordshire Bull Terrier Breed Club Secretaries

Alyn & Deeside
Mr Tony Moran,
12 The Hawthorns,
Audenshaw,
Manchester,
M34 5LU
Tel: 0161 320 6485

Downlands
Mrs Ann Gatenby,
Nettle Cottage,
Privett, Alton,
Hants,
GU34 3PF
Tel: 01730 828402

East Anglian
Mrs Lesley McFadyen,
98 Eastfield Road,
Waltham Cross,
Herts
EN8 7EX
Tel: 01992 427698

East Midlands
Mrs Norma Vann,
The Racings,
14 Chapel Lane,
Gaddesby,
Leics LE7 4WB
Tel: 01664 840570

Merseyside
Mr R Blackley,
54 Victoria Road,
Liverpool,
L13 8AW
Tel: 0151 287 6822

Morecambe Bay & Cumbria
Mr George Earle,
Lingley Bank,
Bothel,
Carlisle,
CA5 2JG
Tel: 01697 320217

North East
Miss Jaci McLauchlan,
8 Darcy Close,
Yarm,
Cleveland
TS15 9TA
Tel: 01642 783948

Northern Counties
Mrs Clare Lee,
Orchard House,
Hazelheads Lane,
Knaresborough,
Yorkshire
HG5 0NX
Tel: 01423 863829

Northern Ireland
Mr T Wildridge,
28 Ballyhill Lane,
Nutts Corner,
Crumlin,
Co. Antrim
BT29 4YP
Tel: 02980 825772

North of Scotland
Miss JA Smith,
18 William Mackie Avenue,
Stonehaven,
Aberdeen
AB39 2PQ
Tel: 01569 760418

North West
Miss S Houghton,
271 twist Lane,
Leigh,
Lancs
WN7 4EH
Tel: 01942 708161

Notts & Derby
Mrs J Smith,
Four Winds,
55 Brackley Gate,
Morley,
Derbyshire
DE7 6DJ
Tel: 01332 781062

Potteries
Mrs Sheila reader,
82 Stanier Street,
Newcastle Under Lyme,
Staffs
ST5 2SY
Tel: 01782 611514

Scottish
Mr George Fleming,
115 Dunira Street,
Tollcross,
Glasgow
G32 8PQ
Tel: 0141 763 2349

South wales
Mr John Holle,
22 Heol y Gors,
Townhill,
Swansea
Tel: 01792 542606

Southern Counties
Mr K Meneer,
Jamina,
The Street,
Steeple,
Essex
CM0 7RH
Tel: 01621 773513

Staffordshire Bull Terrier Club
Mr Jim Beaufoy,
Wyrefare Cottage,
Yew Tree Lane,
Bewdley,
Worcs
DY12 2PJ
Tel: 01299 403382

Western
Mr M Grimwood,
36 Cwrdy Road,
Griffith Town,
Pontypool,
Monmouthshire
NP4 5AG
Tel: 01495 759254

INDEX